Priestless
Parishes

Priestless Parishes

The Baptized Leading the Baptized

Virginia Stillwell

ThomasMore®
– An RCL Company –
Allen, Texas

NIHIL OBSTAT:
Rev. Msgr. Glenn D. Gardner, J.C.D.
Censor Librorum

IMPRIMATUR:
† Most Rev. Charles V. Grahmann
Bishop of Dallas

December 7, 2001

The Nihil Obstat and Imprimatur are official declarations that the material reviewed is free of doctrinal or moral error. No implication is contained therein that those granting the Nihil Obstat and Imprimatur agree with the contents, opinions, or statements expressed.

Acknowledgments
The Scripture quotations contained herein are from the New Revised Standard Version Bible: Catholic Edition copyright © 1993 and 1989 by the Division of Christian Education for the National Council of the Churches of Christ in the U.S.A. Used by permission. All rights reserved.

Send all inquiries to:
Thomas More® Publishing
An RCL Company
200 East Bethany Drive
Allen, Texas 75002-3804

Telephone: 800-264-0368 / 972-390-6300
Fax: 800-688-8356 / 972-390-6560

Visit us at: **www.thomasmore.com**
Customer Service E-mail: **cservice@rcl-enterprises.com**

Printed in the United States of America

Library of Congress Control Number: 2001 13494

7481   ISBN 0-88347-481-6

1 2 3 4 5   05 04 03 02 01

~: *C*ONTENTS :~

∴ Introduction ∾

Where's Father?
The Baptized Leading the Baptized

Two years ago, while I was interning as a hospital chaplain with five other divinity students of different denominations, one of my colleagues spoke seven words that still ring in my ears. She had become Catholic when she married but, since her divorce, had found a home in the Evangelical Free Church where she was now seeking ordination. One day I had told this group about my difficulties praying with patients and she said: "Oh, that's right. You Catholics don't really pray with one another, do you? You leave that up to the priests."

At the time I felt a little insulted and reacted defensively: "Of course we pray with one another!"

But since then I have often heard the echo of her words: "You leave that up to the priests!"

I hear them when Catholics rely on "Father" to do something they could and should do themselves.

I hear them when parishioners ask: "Are you sure it's okay with Father?" or the homebound ask their lay parish visitors: "Where's Father?"

I hear them loud and clear when I doubt my own authority or ability as a baptized Catholic Christian.

In my head her voice offers a counterpoint to the voice of my own father, who asked me years ago: "Why would you study theology? That's priests' work."

What is priests' work? And what is the work of all the baptized?

ᴣᴐ

*I*n dioceses all around the United States, bishops are appointing qualified lay Catholics to lead "priestless" parishes. These laypeople are doing and deciding things that Catholics used to "leave up to the priests." And all around the world, Catholics, many of them priests and bishops, are saying: "That's priests' work!" This phenomenon overturns our most basic assumptions about priesthood, power, and authority in the Catholic Church.

Could this be the beginning of the end of the church as we know it? Is it a revolution in the making?

If it is a revolution, it appears to be Spirit-driven and Spirit-guided. The "good news" is that parishes led by lay Catholics are thriving. With lay leaders as role models and guides, more and more Catholics are claiming the full scope of their authority as baptized Catholic Christians and depending less and less on "Father" to tell them what to do. Priests continue to play a vital role in these parishes, but the responsibility for carrying out the mission of the church is placed squarely where it belongs—in the baptized. While in theory this is exactly what the ordained want and strive for, to foster "the common priesthood of the faithful," in reality it can be both confusing and frightening for a brotherhood of men who are accustomed to a more central, more powerful place in parish life.

It can be just as frightening for a parish. When a Catholic community is told they will not be assigned a priest, it doesn't sound like "good news." It may sound like a death knell or a penance. It may bring grief or embarrassment, anger or fear. When parish lay ministers realize that a layperson will be their boss, they can feel threatened. And you can be sure that a layperson thinks twice before accepting an appointment to lead a Catholic parish.

This book tells the story of lay Catholics who are leading parishes without resident priest-pastors. Each chapter begins with a conversation between people whose lives are affected by this ministry. The situations are true in content if not in details and the cast of characters is typical though fictitious. They are based on my experience in a parish with a lay leader and interviews with eleven lay parish leaders and four diocesan coordinators around the United States. Direct quotes from lay parish leaders, parishioners, priests, and diocesan personnel form the bulk of these eight conversations.

Their words provide answers to common fears and questions about lay parish leaders. Each chapter explores a key issue for ordinary Catholics that is illuminated by their experience and ends with questions to consider. Chapter by chapter, we will discover that lay parish leaders are leading *all* the baptized to claim the grace, vocation, authority, activities, equality, collaboration, and communion that they share through baptism. A concluding chapter names unresolved concerns about this ministry and asks what every Catholic—lay and ordained—can learn from the ministry of lay parish leaders.

Not everything in this story is "good news." These conversations reflect the resistance as well as the support, the challenges as well as the successes, encountered by lay parish leaders and the parishes and dioceses that welcome them. Theirs is not an easy road. They are, as they call themselves, "pioneers," who are breaking the trail as they go, clearing away centuries of thicket. But their enthusiasm is contagious. They are guiding ordained and lay Catholics to rediscover together the power and authority of baptism that they hold in common.

There is plenty of work to do in the church, most of which Catholics no longer must or even should "leave up to the priests." I hope that this book gives courage to those involved with the ministry of lay parish leadership—bishops, diocesan personnel, priests, deacons, lay ministers, parishioners, and lay parish leaders themselves. Even more so, I hope that it encourages all Catholics to claim the full scope of their abilities and authority as members of the baptized.

I am grateful to those who labored with me to bring this book to birth, especially Dr. Kathleen Cahalan and the faculty of Saint John's

University School of Theology and Seminary in Collegeville, Minnesota, and Sister Amy Hoey at the USCCB Office of Family, Laity, Women and Youth. My deepest appreciation goes to those who allowed me to interview them and share their lives. Many prefer to remain anonymous. I am proud to publicly thank Jay Gilchrist, Amy Giorgio, Sister Marilyn Gottemoeller, R.S.M., Carol L. Johnson, Tom Johnson, Father Bill Kenney, Father Dennis Labat, Sister Carol Loughney, Christine Ramirez, Kristin Roth, and the people of Our Lady of Mount Carmel Parish in Minneapolis.

While I made every effort to represent their experience and perspective accurately, I ask their indulgence for the artistic license I took with their words. Through them I have come to understand that the Spirit is indeed efficaciously present in the phenomenon of the baptized leading the baptized. I am grateful to all of them for their candor as well as their love for, fidelity and tireless commitment to the church.

CHAPTER 1

What Priest Shortage?
Abundant Grace

The only thing remarkable about Saints Perpetua and Felicity Parish was that there was nothing remarkable about it. I half expected to see bricks crumbling, mourners veiled in black, and the glum faces of roughly a dozen diehards when I arrived for Mass on Sunday. Instead I heard, before I saw, the crowd of parishioners laughing together outside the church and in the parish office. The smell of coffee brewing and the sight of outstretched hands greeted me as I stepped down into the parish hall. All seemed eager to welcome me, telling me how proud they are of their parish. Was I in the right place? Was this the parish where Denise Garcia had been assigned as "pastoral administrator" when their pastor retired? Sister Charlotte at the diocesan ministry office had told me that this parish was "dwindling"—just too small for the diocese to be able to justify sending them a priest as pastor. Priests, it seems, are getting to be a hot commodity, one that needs to be apportioned wisely.

It had taken me a few seconds to recover when Sister Charlotte first told me that the diocese had a laywoman leading a parish. Had things gotten that bad? The "priest shortage" really meant nothing to me; I had no idea that it had come this close to home.

"Oh yes," Sister Charlotte said offhandedly. "In our diocese we now have over 750,000 Catholics served by 226 priests—that's one priest for every 3,400 Catholics. We have six to eight priests retiring every year and we feel blessed if we have three newly ordained. Of course, the new priests aren't ready to be pastors right away, but we try to train them as associate pastors in a year or two. And the diocese isn't getting any smaller, you know. Old parishes in the cities and rural areas don't disappear when people move to the suburbs and start new parishes. We have more parishes now than we have ever had in the diocese and fewer priests than we've had in over forty years."

I wasn't comprehending this. "I thought the diocese was in control of all that. Don't you folks decide what parishes stay open, who can retire?"

"Yes and no. Sure, the bishop can ask the priests to keep pastoring past the age of seventy, their retirement age, but the priests have said that they are very unhappy with this answer to the problem. These days, very few priests occupy offices like mine, that's for sure; instead, most have parishes. We don't open new suburban parishes unless we absolutely have to, and we have a thousand-person minimum seating requirement for all new church construction to limit the number of Sunday Masses that will need to be celebrated.

"We can close downtown parishes like Saints Perpetua and Felicity. It has dwindled so in numbers and there are five other Catholic parishes within walking distance. But no one wants their parish closed. It's even harder in rural areas where parishes are miles apart. Everyone thinks some other parish should be closed instead of theirs. It feels like such a failure—like a death in the family. The bishop has said he will not close any parish as long as it meets the criteria for financial viability set by the diocesan pastoral council, but some may not last long. Some bishops are doing lots of clustering. We could cluster these six parishes under one or two pastors, but neither the priests nor the people like this idea."

"Does it matter?"

"Yes, of course, it matters. For seven years we have been holding regional meetings of parish representatives in their area. We started by talking about clustering their parishes because of the priest shortage, but there was such an uproar! Each parish has an ethnic identity and so much history.

"Then we proposed that the parishes share their collections and be administrated as one entity while retaining individual pastors. Only one of them currently operates in the black. The priests practically mutinied. Now we are simply trying to facilitate shared ministries among those parishes and collaboration between pastors in the deanery. Even that's a struggle. It's one thing to have the authority to close or cluster parishes. It's another to work out solutions that respect people's lives of faith and offer them the pastoral care they deserve."

"What about hiring missionary priests?"

"Well, some dioceses do that, and some of the priests here think that it's a good idea, but we have been reluctant. Missionary priests come with their own problems. Besides language issues, they don't really understand American culture or how things work in American parishes. It's again a question of meeting people's real pastoral needs. Sometimes a missionary priest can meet their sacramental needs, but in terms of preaching and pastoral care and relating to people, there can be a gap."

"But, Charlotte, can't we just tough it out until the priest numbers start to increase?"

Sister Charlotte's exasperation with me was beginning to show. "Look, we are doing everything we can to advertise and encourage prayer for vocations to the priesthood. And we're not ordaining women or married men anytime soon, if that's what you mean. But even if we had huge increases in the number of seminarians, which we don't foresee, the number of Catholics in the diocese just keeps rising, too.

"There's no getting around it. We're likely to have a dozen or more laypeople and deacons appointed to lead parishes five years from now. The bishop doesn't see as many problems with appointing laypeople to lead parishes as with the other options. Some bishops disagree with him, of course, but he isn't alone in his opinion. The fact is, we can't do only one thing. We have to use every option to try to see that Catholics of the diocese have access to good pastoral care and the sacraments. It could be worse; in some countries the churches are empty.

"Look at it this way. It's a blessing to have so many Catholics in the diocese and so many qualified, committed laypeople like Denise Garcia, who provide leadership for the church. It's a marvelous way of calling forth people's gifts and letting them witness their faith. I believe the life-giving Spirit is at work in this ministry. Just wait. You'll see what I mean."

ふ

*A*s this typical and informative conversation illustrates, the priest shortage is affecting almost every diocese in the United States. Bishops are utilizing every available response in an effort to minimize its effects. Some responses are more effective than others in providing Catholics the pastoral care and sacramental leadership they deserve. Among these responses is the appointment of laypeople to lead parishes. The Catholic Church has less to fear from the appointment of lay leaders than if bishops relied solely on the other options available to them. In fact, the appointment of laypeople to lead parishes is opening windows once more and allowing a breath of fresh air into individual parishes and into the church as a whole.

Fewer Priests

Priests are in shorter and shorter supply these days. One way to gauge the priest shortage is to follow "Sister Charlotte's" lead and look at the changing ratio of priests to Catholics in a given part of the world. In their 1993 study, *Full Pews and Empty Altars: Demographics of the Priest Shortage in United States Catholic Dioceses*, Richard Schoenherr and Lawrence Young say that in 1975 there were 1,102 Catholics per priest in the United States and in 1985 there were 1,374. They estimate that in the year 2005 there will be roughly double the 1975 ratio, with 2,194 Catholics for every functioning priest in the United States (Schoenherr, 1993: 304). Current data from the Center for Applied Research in the Apostolate (CARA) suggest that the U.S.

Catholic population has grown beyond sixty-one million, of whom forty-four million are registered in parishes. This is more than twice the Catholic population reported in *The Official Catholic Directory* for 1951, a time when there were roughly as many active priests in the United States as there are now.

Another way to judge the supply of priests is from the number of parishes that are functioning without resident priests. According to Vatican reports, over 25 percent (54,753) of the world's 216,614 parishes were without resident priests in 1999 (*Annuarium statisticum ecclesiae,* 2001: 63). This year (2001) in the United States, 3,151 of the 19,143 Catholic parishes are without resident priest-pastors. This number represents over 16 percent of parishes nationwide. Thus, one out of every six parishes in the United States is facing the priest shortage directly.

Every section of the country is affected. Last year, the South census division had 431 parishes without resident priests, the Northeast had 390, and the West had 339 "priestless" parishes. While the Midwest section of the country still had the most parishes being served by priests (5,315), it also had the most parishes without resident priest-pastors (1,863). This means that over one in four Midwestern parishes is without a resident priest.

Options Available

Nonresident pastors. What is happening to these parishes? Again, relying on the data from the 2001 *Official Catholic Directory,* 2,241 parishes in the United States (more than one in ten) are functioning with no resident pastoral leader, either lay or ordained. While dioceses in the Southern, Western, and Midwestern regions of the country are appointing nonpriests to lead 25 percent of the parishes that are without resident priests, dioceses in the Northeastern section are currently leaving 92 percent of their "priestless" parishes without any resident pastoral leaders. These parishes may be missions, with no leader providing a pastoral presence and Sunday Mass offered when it can be arranged. They may also be part of a two- or three-parish cluster with a parish that has a pastor. The clustered parishes may or may not have a staff person on site. They receive visits from the nonresident priest on Sundays or one day a week. In many cases the travel and administrative responsibilities involved leave the priest administrator without time or energy for his primary functions of prayer and the "care of souls."

When parishes lack adequate pastoral leadership, people's pastoral needs go largely unmet. Missions and clustered parishes without pastoral leaders usually gather only when a *priest* is present for them to gather *around* at Eucharist. But going to Mass on Sunday is not all there is to parish life. Sunday Mass is meant to refresh and energize the baptized for ministry. Without a pastoral leader in the parish to plan other prayer gatherings, offer formation, facilitate community life, and help them reach out to care for one another and serve the wider community, the ministry of Christ in the parish "dwindles." Neither the parishioners nor the world in which they live experience the presence of Christ living and active in the neighborhood Catholic parish. The reason for the church to exist is to carry on the ministry of Christ. Christ's ministry ought to continue every day in every Catholic parish, whether or not "Father" can be there.

Closings. Other options are plentiful. Many rural and urban parishes have been closed in the last decade purportedly because of lack of available priests. Well over 600 parishes in the United States have been closed in the last two years alone. There are 576 fewer parishes in 2001 than there were in 1999—this despite the creation of roughly seventy new parishes during this period. There may be cases in which closing is the most advisable course of action. However, the real reason for these closings may have been low membership and high debt.

It is difficult to justify most parish closings when we recognize that a Catholic church is meant to serve the whole "parish," or geographic/cultural region in which it is situated, not only the Catholics who are registered, contributing members. To close parishes that are not financially viable is to add the burden of spiritual disadvantage to those already weighed down by economic disadvantage. One strength of the Catholic diocesan system that networks individual congregations "in communion" ought to be that wealthier, stronger parishes support the ministry of Christ in smaller, struggling parishes through diocesan pooling of funds. Parishes should not be closed because of a limited supply of money or priests. Their continuance should depend on the needs of the region and the faith of the Catholic community they serve.

Stretching supply. Several strategies are being employed to stretch the supply of priests. New suburban parishes are encompassing much larger populations and geographic areas than we might expect in one "parish family." Larger churches are being built to accommodate larger assemblies. Many such parishes devote long hours to building community, only to discover that rapid turnover in membership undoes all their best efforts. Rare is the parish with two or three priests, or the priest who has time to visit every family in the parish. Roman collars no longer predominate in diocesan offices and Catholic schools and hospitals, a situation that many Catholics lament. For their part, many priests lament being overburdened by multiple, and multiplying, assignments.

Permanent deacons. Permanent deacons are often utilized to lead parishes, even when they feel called to the work of charity and service instead. In some of the 108 dioceses in the United States that now have the permanent diaconate, deacons are required to earn master's degrees in ministry, whereas in others they receive only a few years of ungraded pastoral and theological formation to supplement their previous work experience and education. Currently half of the permanent deacons in the United States have graduate degrees of some kind, but a third do not even have undergraduate college degrees (Wood, 2000: 148). Even so, some bishops favor appointing reluctant, ill-prepared permanent deacons to lead parishes in lieu of dedicated laypeople. Factors such as motivation, theological credentials, and pastoral experience are not necessarily considered. The most common reason is that deacons can preach on Sundays and preside at baptisms, marriages, and funerals, all of which are functions laypeople can perform with their bishop's permission.

Priests' retirement. With the average age of priests in the United States at fifty-nine and rising, priests are being expected to work as long as they can stand up—or longer. Bishop John Myers, in a pastoral letter to the diocese of Peoria, Illinois, issued June 13, 2001, said that the diocese "needs every priest who is willing to serve." He encouraged priests to "remain in full-time assignments until age seventy-five and thereafter on a year-by-year basis," reminding them of the "salary increases and other financial bonuses for those who keep working past age seventy." He also asked them to consider remaining in the diocese after retirement as "senior priests" who would "continue to serve the church of Peoria in some mutually agreed-upon way," which might include assignment to a small parish or helping at other parishes (*Origins*, July 19, 2001: 164).

While some healthy, elderly priests may eagerly offer to work until the day they die, many bishops are hesitant to ask this of men who have already given fifty years of their lives to the church. Other priests see retirement as a matter of justice to the clergy as well as a wake-up call to the church. They believe that their continuing to function as priests would merely mask the priest shortage and delay the church's response to the problem.

Recruiting. All of us have experienced the prayers and advertising campaigns for priestly vocations—some very respectful of the vocations of women and married men. Some offend without deliberately intending to do so. One bishop says every year: "If I had a hundred lives to live, I would live them all as a priest." The obvious question that arises from the women of the diocese is: "What would you do with your priestly vocation during the fifty-one lives in which you would be born female?"

Numbers of seminarians have risen slightly from a few years ago. However, as Donald Cozzens' *The Changing Face of the Priesthood* suggests, this might be attributed to lower admission standards and less rigorous criteria to discern a candidate's vocation for, or impediments to, the ordained priesthood.

Missionary priests. The effort to recruit missionary priests is very strong in some dioceses, bringing missionaries from Third World countries who are delighted to come to America to live out their priestly career or retirement years. Currently, 16 percent of priests in the United States came from other countries according to a new study sponsored by the bishops' committee on priestly life and ministry. "Sister Charlotte" already told us about the pastoral problem with missionary priests often not understanding American culture and not being able to relate to lay Catholics in the context of American parish life.

However, there is another serious problem with missionary priests. On April 25, 2001, the Congregation for the Evangelization of Peoples issued an *Instruction* approved by the pope. It asks bishops to set strict time limits for visits by clergy to foreign dioceses. The document says that clergy from developing countries often spend many years abroad because of "the higher living conditions which these countries offer and the need for young priests in some of the established churches" (*Origins*, July 19, 2001: 170).

Cardinal Jozef Tomko, retiring head of the congregation, said there is a danger of mission territories being depleted of priests, since some have as many as half of their native clergy abroad, according to the *Catholic News Service*. Cardinal Tomko expressed concern that First World bishops not take the "easy solution" of filling their need for priests without thinking of the damage that can be done to native Third World dioceses, where ratios of Catholics to priests can be as high as 17,500 to 1.

So it seems that every response to the priest shortage has its drawbacks. Appointing lay Catholics to lead parishes is no different. A Vatican document from 1997, the *Instruction on Certain Questions Regarding the Collaboration of the Non-Ordained in the Sacred Ministry of Priests*, issued jointly by eight Vatican congregations, expressed serious concern about whether the distinct identity of the ordained priesthood might be "eroded" and the priesthood of the faithful obscured when nonordained Catholics take on functions normally performed by clergy. It stated a strong preference for using all other possible means of responding to the shortage of priests before utilizing laypeople (Practical Provisions, Article 4, #1b).

This is exactly what the United States bishops are doing. They are utilizing every option available to them, despite the undesirable consequences that each involves. Many now feel they cannot afford to let fears about protecting their own priestly identity stand in the way of providing Catholics with the pastoral and sacramental care they deserve. In order to do so, more and more American bishops are turning to committed, qualified laypeople to share in the pastoral leadership of diocesan parishes.

Appointment of Laypersons

Who is a layperson? The term "laity" is used in various ways. In common usage it refers to Christians who are neither vowed religious nor ordained. However, the word itself means "the people" and originally was applied to all Christians. In church law, the term "lay" refers to all who are baptized but not ordained. This is clear in *The Code of Canon Law*, which divides "Part I: The Christian Faithful" into three categories: "The Obligations and Rights of All the Christian Faithful," "The Obligations and Rights of the Lay Faithful," and "Sacred Ministers or Clerics" (Beal., 2000: v). This book follows canon law and uses the term "lay" to include both those who are and those who are not members of religious orders, but are not ordained. These lay Catholics are being appointed to collaborate with the priests of their dioceses in exercising pastoral care for parishes.

How widespread is this practice? More and more United States dioceses are entrusting priestless parishes to nonordained Catholics. In its recently released *Study of the Impact of Fewer Priests on the Pastoral Ministry*, the bishops' committee on priestly life and ministry reports that 53 percent of dioceses say they expect to substantially increase utilization of nonpriests to lead parishes in the next ten years. The American bishops also found that most ordinary Catholics in the United States favor using deacons and lay people to lead parishes over any other response to the reduced availability of priests.

Where are they being appointed? In the year 2000 one in every twenty-five parishes in the United States—782 of the 19,008 total parishes—was in the care of nonpriests (deacons, teams, or lay-persons). This represents almost four times the 210 such parishes that were reported a decade ago. In the Northeast region the increase is even more dramatic. There, the number of parishes headed by nonpriests has increased eightfold. Lay Catholics now lead 627 of the priestless parishes nationwide, according to statistics in the latest *Official Catholic Directory.* This means that approximately fifty lay leaders have been appointed every year since 1990. The Midwest region has by far the most lay people leading parishes, 433 (69 percent of the 627). The Western region has 89 (14.2 percent), the South has 78 (12.4 percent), and the Northeast region has 27 (4.3 percent).

How does it work? In the parish, the layperson provides pastoral lead-ership while a priest acts as "sacramental minister." Another priest is named to "direct the pastoral care" of the parish, but usually this priest-director has no connection with parish life. As the bishop's delegate, the lay leader holds decision-making authority in the parish, always in subordination to the bishop. Many of these parishes are small rural communities that would otherwise not have anyone to offer a pastoral presence in the area. Sometimes a lay leader is a parish's only option to closing. More and more, however, urban and suburban parishes are also having laypeople appointed to lead them.

Historical Precedents

It is an old solution to an old problem. Whenever an organizational "body" grows too large for one "head," the responsibilities of the leader are shared with more and more people. We see it in the devel-opment of middle management in American corporate bodies and we see it in the history of the Body of Christ as it grew from a tiny sect into the worldwide megaconglomerate that it is today.

Scripture. This phenomenon can be discovered at work even in the Gospels. Early in his ministry Jesus sees that "the harvest is plentiful, but the laborers are few" (Matthew 9:37). Out of compassion for the people who are "like sheep without a

shepherd" (Matthew 9:36), Jesus sends out the Twelve to extend his
pastoral ministry (Matthew 10:1). Later, on being told that the
thousands of disciples around him are famished, he challenges the
Twelve: "You give them something to eat" (Matthew 14:16;
Mark 6:37; Luke 9:13). He alone cannot feed the hordes, but with the
help of the apostles, his collaborators, Jesus' power to nourish is
extended to every hungry mouth. As his ministry continues, Jesus
sends not just the Twelve, but seventy-two other disciples to carry his
ministry of healing and message of good news ahead of him (Luke
10:1, 8–9). At the Gospels' end, Jesus' disciples are sent to "make
disciples of all nations" (Matthew 28:19), even "to the ends of the
earth" (Acts 1:8).

The Acts of the Apostles depicts in broad strokes the exponential
growth among followers of the way. The expansion begins at
Pentecost when the Spirit anoints not only the apostles but 120
disciples with power (Acts 1:15). As the church grows, the Twelve
maintain pastoral responsibility for "prayer and serving the word,"
while appointing seven Hellenistic disciples who were "full of the
Spirit and of wisdom" (Acts 6:3, 4) to do what the apostles could
not—care for the needs of the Hellenistic Jewish church and its
mission to non-Jews (Acts 6:1–7). The Twelve, like Jesus, can't attend
to all the needs of the church alone. Nor are they, as Hebrews, well
equipped to care for the Hellenistic church. Thus, they share pastoral
responsibility for the life of the burgeoning Christian community.
The Twelve also recognize the power of the Spirit working in Paul
(Acts 9:27, 28), and bless his extension of the ministry of Christ to the
gentiles (Acts 15:6–29). Because the apostles share pastoral responsibility for the church with Paul and the Hellenists, the ministry of
Christ reaches all the way to Rome.

Paul himself knows that he cannot take complete responsibility
for the churches he founds. He, too, entrusts leadership responsibilities to various members of the Christian community in the cities he
visits (1 Corinthians 16:15–18). While he is absent, which is the great
majority of the time, these coworkers guide and care for the faith of
the communities entrusted to them. Jesus, the Twelve, and Paul

trusted the Holy Spirit enough to share pastoral responsibility for the church with others. Without their courage and responsiveness to what the Spirit was doing in the church, Christianity might still be a tiny sect of Judaism, one that we know little or nothing about.

Early church. As the period represented in the scriptures drew to a close, "presbyters" and "bishops" appear to have shared leadership of the churches. In her book, *Sacramental Orders*, Susan K. Wood outlines how the order of presbyters, those we now commonly call priests, developed over the next three centuries (Wood, 2000, pp. 117–118). During the second century, a system of leadership took hold in which a bishop would "oversee" the life of each local church community, its baptisms, and its Eucharist. A council of presbyters, or presbyteral council, advised the bishop. Deacons helped the bishop care for the community. Originally, the presbyters could not baptize or preside at Eucharist on their own.

However, as the Spirit swelled the ranks of Christians in the third and fourth centuries, local churches grew too large and scattered to gather in one place around a bishop's table for the Eucharist. New responsibilities were delegated by the bishop to his council of presbyters. They were gradually given responsibility for presiding at the Eucharist, baptizing and absolving penitents at the various gatherings of Christians around the region (parishes). Even so, they were still, and are today, understood to be collaborating together with the bishop in the exercise of the bishop's pastoral responsibility as the shepherd and priest of the local church, the diocese.

Present day. The church is seeing a similar development in the resurgence of the permanent diaconate today. Many hope that priests will be able to share their sacramental and pastoral responsibilities with permanent deacons. And yet deacons are not ordained to priesthood but to service, the literal meaning of the Greek word *diakonia*. Originally, their role was not to help priests; it was to help the bishop in the work of charity in the local church.

Over the centuries there has been a continuing tendency to place deacons in sacramental roles. Thus, the church has struggled to maintain the distinct identity of the diaconate as representing and facilitating the church's ministry of service (Wood, 2000, pp. 173–176). History teaches that permanent deacons alone cannot and should not be expected to fill the pressing needs for pastoral and sacramental care in the church today.

The United States Bishops' Committee on the Laity sums up the history of ministry in the church in their 1999 report *Lay Ecclesial Ministry:* "Throughout the history of the church, the hierarchy has been responsible for ordering its ministries. The official ministries vary in response to needs that change over time" (19). The report urges bishops today to continue this pattern "in faithfulness to the apostolic tradition and in response to the community's needs" (20). It invites them to respond both to the needs of their local church and to what the Spirit is doing in their time and place as they "order" appropriate ministries for their people today.

One of the church's needs to which bishops are invited to respond is the short supply of priests. A second and more pressing problem is the number of Catholic communities who deserve but are doing without pastoral leadership. One of the works of the Spirit is the growing number of Catholics in the United States. Another gift of the Spirit is the profusion of laypeople who are called to and gifted for ministries in the church. The appointment of laypeople to collaborate with the bishop and priests of a diocese in providing pastoral leadership to priestless parishes is a response to both the needs of our time and the work of the Spirit in the church. It follows a long tradition of leaders sharing pastoral responsibility for the church with qualified members of the Christian community.

Be Not Afraid

Is there a shortage of priests in the United States church today? That depends on how we look at it. How many priests are enough priests? *The Catechism of the Catholic Church* states that the ordained priesthood "is at the service of the common priesthood. It is directed at the unfolding of the baptismal grace of all Christians" (#1547). How many priests does the church of the twenty-first century need to unfold "the baptismal grace of all Christians?" On the one hand, many bishops from around the world would envy our abundance. One diocese in Kenya has parishes with 20,000 parishioners and a total of twenty-four priests for its 350,000 Catholics—one for every 17,500 people.

On the other hand, the situation in the United States has changed drastically over the last two decades. There are many more Catholics per priest than in the past and this ratio is likely to increase rapidly as older priests retire. Priests are working longer and harder, traveling to many churches in a single day, or celebrating Mass in enormous congregations filled with anonymous faces. There are not enough priests to pastor all Catholic parishes, nor even enough to provide for everyone's sacramental needs.

Every diocese in the United States, if not yet every parish, feels the pinch. Every American Catholic will soon experience the effects of the declining numbers of priests. They may hear of parish closings. The Catholic high school may not have a priest on staff. The pastor may be replaced, but not the associate. The new pastor may also be expected to serve a "mission" parish—or two. And, sooner rather than later, they or a neighboring parish may be assigned a layperson to provide pastoral leadership in place of a priest. Things have gotten *"that bad."*

Or have they? There is another way to view this situation. We may be suffering not so much from a shortage of priests as from an abundance of grace. We have more Catholics in America than ever before in our history and more laypeople qualified to provide pastoral leadership in the church than we could have even imagined at the time of the Second Vatican Council. In *Lay Ecclesial Ministry*, the bishops agree that "Lay ecclesial ministry is a gift of the Spirit to the church. The experience of the past thirty-five years can be seen as the grace-filled work of the Spirit" (20). Some people even consider the decreasing number of available priests to be a blessing, since it is making room for others to use their gifts in service and leadership to the church.

While not everyone agrees with this last statement, there is broad agreement with "Sister Charlotte" that the grace of the Spirit is expanding our numbers and equipping the church with laypeople who are called and gifted for pastoral leadership.

The next chapter will explore more fully the call and qualifications of lay parish leaders. Our current situation calls for bishops to tap into these gifts to provide pastoral care to American Catholics, lest they go elsewhere to have their needs met. Parishes do not have to fear receiving lay leaders instead of priests; they are more than qualified. Bishops do not have to be afraid to share pastoral responsibilities with other members of the Body of Christ; it has been done before.

When bishops who are faced with a diminishing supply of priests appoint lay Catholics to lead parishes in their dioceses, they are acting in a long line of courageous leaders who did what was necessary so that the ministry of Christ could continue in the church. They are recognizing that the Spirit is working in the church to call and equip laymen and laywomen for pastoral leadership, and they are utilizing this gift. They are responding to the miraculous catch of fish in their nets by "signal[ing] their partners . . . to come and help them" keep the large population of American Catholics in the barque of Peter (Luke 5:6, 7). They are not allowing the ministry of Christ to be shackled by anyone's memories of yesterday or fears for tomorrow. They are extending their pastoral reach by sharing responsibility for the pastoral care of the church with qualified disciples, a tradition that goes back to Jesus himself.

Questions to Consider

- How have you experienced the effects of the limited supply of priests in the United States?
- What worries or saddens you about the declining numbers of priests?
- What "solutions" has your diocese tried? How have people responded?
- Is the appointment of lay parish leaders a traditional or a radical step? Explain.
- What concerns or excites you about laypeople leading parishes?

CHAPTER 2

Are Laypeople Qualified to Lead Parishes?
Baptismal Vocation

*I*n the shower that Sunday morning, Denise remembered that she had scheduled an interview after church. The interviewer had asked to talk with her about her experience as a pastoral administrator.

"What'll I say?" she thought, and her mind drifted back through these three eventful years to the conversation that began it all. . . .

"Denise Garcia? The bishop will see you now."

As she was led down the hall to the bishop's office, Denise had tried to hold terror at bay with her current mantra, "Here I am, Lord. I come to do your will." She had to remind herself to breathe.

"Good morning, Bishop. Thank you for agreeing to see me."

"Good morning, Denise. I've been looking forward to meeting you ever since I received your letter. Father Warren speaks very highly of you. Please sit down." His warm smile, direct gaze, and handshake felt like lifelines.

"I understand you want to offer your services to lead parishes that don't have resident priests. There are several in the diocese now. I feel strongly that we should have a pastoral leadership presence—priest or otherwise—in every parish that can financially support one. Currently, we have six people serving as pastoral administrators—a deacon and five laypeople, two of whom are religious sisters. It seems to be working well, considering the challenges to everyone involved."

"I'm so glad to hear that."

"I'm curious about what motivated you to approach me regarding this ministry."

"It was a difficult decision for me. I've been working in this diocese for twenty-some years and have developed a certain sense of responsibility for the faith of the people here. I know of the trouble you're having in finding priests to serve all your parishes. I also recognize that I have gifts that could serve the needs of parishes without priest-pastors. Over the past year, I've prayed a lot about this and talked to Father Warren. Gradually, with the help of my spiritual director and my family, I have discerned that I was being called to offer my services to you. After all, the church needs everyone's gifts."

"Certainly, we can use every gift that laypeople have to offer. God's call to each is unique and good and we believe that it is given for the good of the church. Ordained people have gifts but not all the gifts! You say your family helped you decide. They support you in this?"

"Very much so. My children are grown and don't live with us. And my husband has a business here in the city, so we intend to stay here. He understands the stresses of pastoral ministry. I've had heavy responsibilities at Saint Jude's these past few years and he has provided tremendous support to me."

"Would you tell me a little bit about your experiences in ministry?"

"Well, right now I'm the pastoral associate at Saint Jude's. I've worked with two different pastors in my seven years there. Together we've gone through closing the school, a capital campaign, and church renovation. They've been hard years, but wonderful learning experiences. Before that, I served in various parish ministries in different parishes for about twelve years. During all this time, I've tried to keep current with conferences and training in different aspects of ministry to supplement my Master of Divinity degree. Previously, I taught at Holy Spirit High School for several years. I was also in the novitiate with the Notre Dame sisters for a year after high school and I grew up Catholic, volunteering for whatever came along."

"That's quite a range and depth of experience. As you surely know, we look for folks with master's degrees and professional experience. It's not so much the education as the life experience that's important. Our pastoral administrators generally get their training by serving as pastoral associates. So you're definitely qualified to be a pastoral administrator; in many ways you are more qualified than some of our priests. Why do you want to leave Saint Jude's for the struggles of leading a parish?"

"I can't say that I do. But I feel called to this ministry. I have leadership gifts and good community-building skills and I feel called to use them. It feels like I was meant to do this in service to God and the people. I just know it's where God wants me to be."

"Ah. I see that your Master of Divinity is from Saint Columba's. An excellent credential. How did you happen to go there?"

"As I said, I was teaching then, and I had some prayer experiences that really deepened my relationship with God. I felt a strong calling to study theology and to, I guess you'd say, spread the good news about God's love. Anyway, at first I resisted because I didn't think we could manage finances or child care with me in school. So I entered the lay ministry formation program here in the diocese. But I needed more, and my husband was determined we could make it work. So that's what we did."

"It sounds like your whole family made quite a sacrifice."

"I appreciate your saying that. It was a sacrifice for all of us, but I received much more than I gave up. Now I have the education and the experience to go with my call. All three feel like gifts I want to give back to the church."

"For my part I regret that we haven't yet implemented ways to financially support people like you who are called to ministry but can't be ordained. And I thank you and your family for all you have given the church over the years."

"You're welcome, Bishop. What can I say? It would help at least to be affirmed publicly for my gifts."

"If it were open to you, would you like to be ordained?"

"Now that sounds like a loaded question! No, I don't want to be a priest. I know there are people who do and I'm sorry they feel that being ordained would be better than what I have. Pastoral care and the nurturing of a community's faith life is very rewarding work. Pardon me, Bishop, but I feel freer without ordination. I don't feel limited by who I'm not. I believe lay leaders are showing the holiness to which all the baptized are called, regardless of ordination, celibacy, or whatever. I show people that our life of faith is something that we are all called to, that it isn't so distant. We all have a vocation to follow God."

"It seems to me that God has gifted lots of different people with vocations and leadership skills, Denise, and we must steward those gifts wisely. I believe that this ministry is the work of the Holy Spirit. It may be a whole flowering of something new—like monasticism was—in the life of the church. I'm glad you took the initiative and came to see me. I'll be meeting with the pastoral personnel board next week. I'll talk with them about your interest and qualifications. If you don't hear from them within the month, please call my secretary. Thank you, Denise, for offering your services to the diocese."

"Thank you for your time, Bishop." Denise shook his hand, turned to walk down the hall, and took a deep, deep breath.

ॐ

*D*enise's character typifies laypeople who lead Catholic parishes in the United States. Who are they? How did they get there? What qualifications do they have?

To begin with, they are not ordained; they are "merely" baptized. They come from every walk of life. They are people of prayer who feel called to place their gifts at the service of the people of God. They have given innumerable volunteer hours to their parishes. Most have paid for their own ministry degrees. Their formation and education have prepared them for leadership. Their experience in ministry has matured them. Their skills, personal traits, and knowledge qualify them to lead. And their proven dedication to the church allows their bishops to trust them with the pastoral care of parishes. These Catholics are not allowing themselves to be limited by their lack of ordination. What qualifies them for leadership in the church is that they have responded fully to the holiness, the gifts and the vocation of baptism.

Three significant traits emerge from this quick snapshot of lay parish leaders. First, lay leaders are "merely" baptized and living the holiness therein. Second, they are well qualified by formation, education, and experience. Third, they discern within themselves both the call and the gifts for leadership in the church. A closer look at these three traits will reveal a richer portrait of the vocation to ministry and the vocation of all the baptized.

Merely Baptized

Lay. The term "lay" refers to all nonordained people in the church— that is, the "merely" baptized. This includes married and single men and women and vowed religious sisters and brothers. It includes all ages, ethnic, and socioeconomic groups. Likewise, lay parish leaders of Catholic parishes represent all these backgrounds and walks of life, although most are late middle-aged. They are what we might call ordinary Catholics. Those who were interviewed for this study include two married and two single women, one married and two single men, and four women religious. They range in age from twenty-five to sixty-five and lead parishes in eleven different dioceses across the United States.

Ten years ago the majority of lay parish leaders in the United States were vowed religious women, but this has changed over the last decade. In 1990 there were 129 parishes led by vowed religious women and only nineteen by married or unvowed lay Catholics. In 2000, the number of parishes led by religious sisters had more than doubled, to 296. However, the number led by other laypeople had increased to 313—sixteen times the number from a decade ago. Now only 47 percent of these parishes are being led by vowed religious women, a few are led by vowed religious brothers, and roughly 50 percent are led by married and single laypeople.

What accounts for the change? In the 1980s, most of those who had the credentials, the experience, and the credibility to lead parishes were religious women. They had already had careers in education, administration, and ministry. They were the first group of laity to earn graduate degrees in theology. So they were the first wave of appointees to lead Catholic parishes.

By the 1990s, however, some of these women had left their communities and many other laypeople had obtained theology and ministry credentials. These lay Catholics have worked for ten years or more in parish ministry, diocesan offices, and Catholic education and now have the credibility to receive appointments as lay parish leaders. The range of lifestyles of the lay leaders interviewed illustrates this trend.

Holy. The issue of personal holiness is significant. Catholics expect priest-pastors to be holy. Are these lay leaders holy? Those interviewed utilize various methods of prayer, reflection, formation, and communal support to help them live "holy" lives. Their personal holiness manifests itself in the hardships they are willing to accept for the sake of the gospel, their self-knowledge and maturity, and their ability to care for the people in their charge. And these lay leaders feel their example challenges other lay Catholics to embrace their own call to holiness.

All Catholics are called to foster their personal holiness day by day. While vowed religious deliberately choose this goal when they choose their state of life, other lay Catholics, like "Denise," are also responsible for cultivating holiness in the context of their married and

single lifestyles. Likewise, at every stage of life the baptized are challenged again to rediscover how they are to be holy. Lay parish leaders
show all Catholics that holiness is not simply for the ordained. Even
the merely baptized can, and should, grow more and more holy
throughout their lives.

Adequate Formation

As previously mentioned, in 1997 the Holy See issued the *Instruction
on Certain Questions Regarding the Collaboration of the Non-Ordained in
the Sacred Ministry of Priests.* This *Instruction* calls for bishops to select
laypeople who demonstrate "adequate formation" and "exemplary
moral life" and to provide them with ongoing formation (Practical
Provisions, #13). Recently, the National Association for Lay Ministry
has helped define adequate formation by publishing certification
standards for lay leaders of Catholic parishes and other paid lay
ministers (*Competency-Based Certification Standards for Pastoral
Ministers, Pastoral Associates, Parish Life Coordinators,* National
Association for Lay Ministry, Inc., 1994). Both the Vatican requirement and the standards for certification indicate the importance of
the qualifications of lay parish leaders.

Based on the rich background of the lay leaders who were interviewed, it seems that lay leaders are well qualified for their work. All
but one of the interviewees have earned graduate degrees in theology
or divinity. Most have received spiritual formation in seminary, lay
ministry programs, or religious life. Half have been institutional or
corporate administrators. They average over twenty years in ministry
each. Most had served as pastoral associates in parishes before their
appointments.

Education. Dioceses generally require lay parish leaders to hold a
Master of Arts, Master of Pastoral Ministry, or Master of Divinity
degree. The Master of Arts is more theologically oriented, while the
pastoral ministry degree is more practical. The divinity degree
combines the two in a larger program. This is the same degree that

seminarians earn in preparation for ordination. While dioceses pay for the graduate degrees of priest candidates, for the most part lay Catholics finance their own education.

The common justification for this policy is that, once ordained, priests take a vow of stability in the diocese, whereas lay Catholics can change careers or move away. Yet the United States bishops have raised this issue by asking: "How might the [U.S.] conference assist dioceses in the development of plans for financing the preparation of lay ecclesial ministers?" (*Lay Ecclesial Ministries,* 65). Many examples now exist of payment for education in exchange for a commitment to service. Lay ministers should not have to shoulder the financial burden of their education alone. Even so, their investment in education is another reliable sign of their dedication to the church.

Experience. Dioceses look for people with several years of ministry experience, especially in pastoral care, since this is the focus of a lay parish leader's work. One diocesan coordinator said it is helpful if the layperson has demonstrated some stability in the diocese, as Denise had, by spending several years in a parish position and getting to know priests and others in the diocese. These people can then vouch for the lay minister's personal maturity and commitment to the church. Occasionally, lay parish leaders are chosen from the membership or staff of the parish. Many dioceses also assign lay leaders to yearlong internships under the outgoing pastor before they take responsibility for leading the parish.

Formation. The lay leaders interviewed continue to seek ongoing education, spiritual formation, and emotional support. As the merely baptized, these Catholics do not receive the full benefit of the priestly fraternity to support them; however, many dioceses offer formation and educational meetings for lay parish leaders. Most lay leaders also find support from members of their religious communities, their spouses, family members, spiritual directors, priests, colleagues, and friends. They pay to attend retreats and seminars. As they have throughout their lives of faith, they derive their primary support from worship and relationships in their parish communities.

In short, they find support from the same sources as all of the baptized.

All these qualifications together indicate that lay parish leaders exceed the criteria for adequate formation. In fact, their years of experience and commitment to ongoing education make them more qualified than some of the clergy with whom they interact.

Called and Gifted

As Denise told her fictitious bishop—these lay leaders feel strongly that they have been called to pastoral leadership. They describe lives of prayer and openness that have taught them to hear and respond to the Spirit's voice. Through their ongoing involvement in the Christian community, the Spirit has nurtured their gifts and energized them to extend the ministry of Christ in every way they can. This includes helping the church embrace its mission to bring Christ's ministry into the world. Thus, they describe themselves as both called and gifted for leadership in the church.

This sense of call and giftedness empowers them to pursue courageously the ministry of church leadership. Four of those interviewed initiated their involvement in this ministry by offering their services to their bishops, and four were "pioneers"—the first laypeople to lead parishes in their dioceses. They talk about their vocations compelling them to find ways to use their leadership gifts in the service of Christ's church.

Dioceses can nurture such vocations to ministry and leadership in various ways. Most interviewees said that the support of their bishops has had an immense impact on encouraging laypeople to respond generously to the voice of the Spirit. Some dioceses have developed ways to affirm lay ministers for sharing their gifts with the church. Others provide lay ministry formation programs. Such programs offer introductions to various theological and pastoral subjects without the pressure or expense of college courses. These programs can help lay Catholics discover their gifts and discern how they are called to use them to further Christ's mission in the world.

Vocation without Ordination?

Vocations to ministry. We have said that lay leaders consider themselves to have a vocation to ministry. But can the nonordained, the merely baptized, really have a true vocation to ministry?

Traditionally, Catholics have focused on vocations to the priesthood. They allowed that religious sisters and brothers had a sort of second-class vocation, but surely not other lay Catholics. Through lay parish leaders and all lay ministers Catholics are discovering otherwise. As one diocesan coordinator said: "God has gifted lots of different people with vocations and leadership skills." The ordained do not have a monopoly on vocations to ministry.

History. A few examples from church history will illustrate. Jesus was not a priest who offered sacrifice in the temple. He was not a rabbi who taught in the synagogue. He was not even a scribe—what later history called a "cleric." He was merely an ordinary Jew who claimed his right and responsibility to lead the Jewish people. He responded fully to the calling he received when he was baptized in the Jordan River by placing his miraculous gifts at the service of the people and the Kingdom of God.

Similarly, Saint Paul was merely an ordinary Christian. While later tradition has bestowed on him apostolic rank, in his own time he had no such status. He was not among those who received the Spirit at Pentecost. He never even knew the Lord. And yet he did not hesitate to preach the Good News and guide the churches that formed in response to his preaching. His vocation to ministry flowed immediately from his conversion and baptism. And he was undeterred by the contempt that other Christians felt for him (Acts 9:17–22). In the thirteenth century, Francis of Assisi, a layman, also responded to a profound call to preach, to serve the poor, and to rebuild the church. He called himself and his followers "little brothers," never "fathers." Church history is replete with examples of vocations that had nothing to do with ordination, but everything to do with ministry.

Theology. In *Lay Ecclesial Ministries*, the United States bishops affirm that lay ministers are living out their vocation as baptized Christians since they are, first, responding to an internal call and, second, exercising the gifts of the Spirit given to them in baptism (Committee on the Laity, 1999: 16). And yet, in 1964, the Vatican II *Constitution on the Church* said that the vocation of the laity has a "secular," or worldly, character. "Sacred" ministry, or ministry in the church, was said to be proper to the ordained (*LG*, #31). This suggested that laypeople who work in ministry in the church simply "supply sacred functions to the best of their ability . . . when there are no sacred ministers" (*LG*, #35). Ministry was not seen as a vocation, or calling, of the merely baptized.

The American bishops now soundly dispute such firm boundaries between sacred and secular vocations as being too facile an interpretation for today's circumstances. It is a false dichotomy to say that the baptismal priesthood is exclusively oriented outward toward the world and the ordained priesthood is exclusively oriented inward toward the church. The bishops recognize that every ministry within the church is also a service to the world, since it enables the church to carry out Christ's ministry in the world:

> "[Some] of the laity are called to . . . working in the Church and focusing on the building of ecclesial communion, which has as its purpose the transformation of the world. *Lay ecclesial ministry should not be seen as a retreat by the laity from their role in the secular realm.* Rather lay ecclesial ministry is an affirmation that the Spirit can call the lay faithful to participation in the building of the Church in various ways" (*LEM*, 15, italics added).

Thus, lay ministers in general, and lay parish leaders in particular, are properly living out their own baptismal vocation when they respond to the call to exercise leadership in the church. They are not simply filling in for "Father." They have a true vocation to ministry even though they are not ordained.

Lay ministry. But do they aspire to ordination? While most lay parish leaders who were interviewed say they would welcome the ordination of women and married men, the majority of them made a point of saying that they themselves are not interested in being ordained. This is significant since the 1997 *Instruction* on collaboration expressed concern that lay ministry might be "perceived and lived as an undue aspiration to the ordained ministry" (*Instruction*, Practical Provisions, 1.2). The opposite seems to be the case here. These lay ministers feel called to church leadership by baptism and are acting on this vocation, independent of the church's criteria for ordination.

Even so, lay ministers who lead parishes do receive their bishop's public authorization. In this way the church recognizes their vocation, thanks them for their dedication, and sends them into ministry. Similar official recognition for other lay ministers would be equally valuable both for the lay ministers and for the communities they serve.

Several questions have surfaced in theological circles regarding how the Catholic community supports and affirms lay vocations to ministry. Both theologians and bishops are asking: Why does recruiting for vocations focus entirely on candidates for ordination or religious life? Can recruitment target *all* who feel called to ministry? How can formation and education for lay ministries be better supported? How can the church affirm, thank, and send people for *all* ministries in the Catholic Church—both lay and ordained?

The vocation of Catholics to ministry in the church is neither a departure from the vocation proper to the baptized nor an undue aspiration to ordination. It is a development of the effects of baptism that calls and equips them to participate in leading the church in its efforts to continue the ministry of Christ. Without such a development of the effects of baptism in one's life, no one would be qualified either to minister in the Christian community or to receive ordination. Ultimately, it is not the "excellent credentials," the years of experience, or the proven dedication of lay parish leaders that are most significant. Like Jesus and Paul and Francis before them, their mature, formed Christian vocations are the sine qua non for ministry and leadership in the church.

The Vocation of All the Baptized

What difference does this make for the millions of Catholics who experience no such vocation to ministry? And what of those who do sense a call to ministry, but not as professional lay ministers in the church? Are they to feel less mature or less holy than these lay ecclesial ministers? The lay parish leaders who were interviewed would say a resounding "No!" To follow the lead of the United States bishops cited earlier, all those who, first, respond to an internal call and, second, exercise the gifts of the Spirit in their particular walk of life are living out their vocation as baptized Christians. Two questions arise. First, what is the internal call of all the baptized? Second, what are the gifts of the Spirit that the baptized are called to exercise?

Baptismal call. What is the vocation, the "internal call," of all the baptized? A look at the anointing section of the Rite of Baptism reveals the answer. In baptism each new Catholic Christian is anointed with consecrated chrism that bears the presence of Christ. Since the word "Christ" itself means "anointed one," we could say that every Catholic becomes a "Christ" (an anointed one) when anointed with chrism in baptism. They become immersed (or "baptized") in the real presence of Christ in the Christian community.

In the scriptures, anointing rituals are understood to signify one's purpose or mission. So, the anointing in the Rite of Baptism looks forward to the purpose—or calling—of baptism in the life of the one who is baptized. The words that accompany the anointing explain this purpose: the newly baptized Christian is to be "priest, prophet, and king" as was Christ himself. *All* the baptized have a vocation to "continue the mission and ministry of Christ," the anointed one, who now serves as priest, prophet, and king through the lives of baptized Christians (*Instruction*, Practical Provisions, 1.2). How lay Catholics can exercise this calling will be addressed later. The Spirit calls the whole community of Christians to continue the ministry of Christ the priest, the prophet, and the king however their life circumstances and their gifts allow. This points to our second question.

Baptismal gifts. What are the "gifts of the Spirit" that the baptized are called to exercise? In the parable of the buried talents, Matthew reminds us that our personal talents and wealth are all gifts given to us by the Lord to be used in God's service (Matthew 25:14–30). In the case of lay parish leaders, their gifts for leadership and caregiving are paramount. Following their example, *all* the baptized must discover which gifts they have been given that "are unique and good."

Added to one's particular gifts is the traditional list of the gifts of the Spirit connected with confirmation—the Spirit of wisdom, understanding, counsel, fortitude, knowledge, piety, and fear of the Lord. This list of spiritual gifts comes from the book of Isaiah (11:2). The passage describes the Messiah (the Hebrew word for "anointed one") who will at last be able to bring justice and peace to Israel because: "The Spirit of the Lord shall rest on him." That is, this "Anointed One" will be slathered with the Spirit of God, whose attributes, or gifts, will permeate not only his skin but also his whole being. Christians have always related this messianic identity and these gifts to Jesus, who is called the Messiah, the Christ. Catholics believe that the same messianic Spirit now permeates the whole community of the baptized, which also enjoys the same gifts of the Spirit.

The Christian community calls down this messianic Spirit and these gifts on those who are anointed in the Rite of Confirmation. All those who are anointed with the Spirit of Christ in baptism and confirmation are said to participate, or share, in both Jesus' identity as the Lord's "Anointed One" and in the gifts of the Spirit. As a result, *all* the baptized have a responsibility to nurture the Spirit's gifts in themselves. They are to utilize these gifts to shape the world into the kingdom of the Messiah, a holy place where truth and justice rule and all can live in peace.

The experience of lay leaders in priestless parishes has convinced them that when ordinary Catholics fully embrace their baptismal vocation, others will follow their lead. When ordinary Catholics deliberately seek to nurture holiness in their lives and relationships, when they seek to live out their baptismal calling in their work and society, when they seek to offer their gifts in service to the church and the world, others find the inspiration and the courage to do the same.

Every one of the "merely" baptized has the responsibility to tap deeply into the gifts and call of baptism and confirmation. And they have the power to lead others to participate more fully in the ministry of the Messiah, the Christ.

One diocesan coordinator expressed it well: "All the baptized have a call and gifts, and the church can use them all," whether in professional church work, in volunteer ministries, in family life and relationships, or in the world of work. Sadly, not every Catholic experiences a warm reception for their gifts from church ministers. Like Saint Paul—and like Jesus before him—they may have to exercise their gifts in the face of resistance and rejection. Yet this does not excuse them from the responsibility to follow the Spirit's urgings. The example of lay parish leaders encourages *all* the baptized to discover the Spirit's call and exercise their gifts to continue the ministry of Christ both in the church and in the world. In the next chapter I will explore what gives them the authority to do so.

Questions to Consider

- What gifts should a parish or diocese look for in lay parish leaders?
- Which is more important for a lay parish leader—education, spiritual formation, or experience? Explain.
- Should the church do more to affirm or support lay ministers? If so, what?
- What is the Spirit calling you to learn or to do?
- Do you experience yourself as having a vocation? Explain.
- What gifts do lay Catholics in particular have to offer the church?
- What should lay Catholics do if they feel that neither their call nor their gifts are being utilized in the church?
- How might the church change to better enable all Catholics to fully exercise their baptismal vocation?

⌁ CHAPTER 3 ⌁

Who Authorizes Them?
Apostolic Authority

"Come on in, Sister Charlotte. Thanks for coming. Can I get you a cup of tea?"

"Thanks. That would be nice. Good to see you again, Mr. Lopez." As she sat on a stackable orange office chair, an unsteady hand first poured, then served her a Styrofoam cup of hot water with a Lipton tea bag and plastic spoon.

"Sweetener's here if you like. And please call me Mike. Last night we had kind of a wild pastoral council meeting in this room. I wanted to talk with you about people's reactions right away so I could include your responses when I send the minutes out. That okay with you?"

"Sure. I appreciate your promptness."

"No problem. I just wish I'd known that being pastoral council president would be all work and no glory! Seriously, we need a lot of clarification on this proposal the diocese is making to assign us a layperson instead of a priest. People don't know whether to be embarrassed or angry about it. They think we deserve a priest just like every other parish."

"And of course they're right. They do deserve a priest. But we think lay leaders provide a great opportunity for parishes in situations like yours. They help parishes stay open and active."

"It's just that we've never heard of laypeople running parishes. It doesn't sound Catholic. Can you give me some more details?"

"I'd love to. I brought some information packets on this ministry for you to give the council. But I want to be sure I answer your questions. What do people want to know?"

"Well, first, what would we call the person?"

"There isn't one standard title for this ministry yet. It's difficult since only bishops and priests are given the title "Pastor." In this diocese we call them pastoral administrators. The title doesn't seem all that important. It simply indicates their role. Sometimes, informally, people will call them lay pastors but, technically, that's incorrect."

"Is this legal? I mean, is it okay with Rome for a layperson to run a parish?"

"To provide temporary pastoral care, yes. It's allowed in the 1983 *Code of Canon Law* for bishops to appoint qualified laypersons to parishes when there's a shortage of priests. Some dioceses around the world have been doing this for over twenty years. The decision is up to the local bishop. It's a formal appointment that would be posted in the diocesan newspaper, just as priest appointments are. A priest would also be appointed to direct the pastoral care of your parish. He's called the canonical moderator in our diocese. And one or more priests would celebrate the sacraments with you."

"How much power would the pastoral administrator really have? Maybe the basic question is, 'Would we have to do what they say, like with a priest?'"

"The person responsible for day-to-day life and decisions in the parish would be the bishop's appointee, the pastoral administrator. So, yes, they have the same power as pastors have. However, ultimate authority for the parish would rest in the bishop, as it does when a parish has a priest-pastor. In our diocese the pastoral administrators discuss parish decisions with the canonical moderator. Along with the priests, they follow diocesan policies regarding resources and division of responsibilities. They exercise financial decisions according to diocesan guidelines, again, under the ultimate supervision of the bishop. Still, the pastoral administrator is the top authority in the parish. The priest who is the sacramental minister has no decision-making authority."

"Could we go to the bishop if we didn't like what the person did?"

"Yes, just as you may when you have a priest-pastor, but the bishop's likely to refer you back to the pastoral administrator. All pastoral leaders are directly responsible to the bishop. Pastoral administrators are his delegates and serve at his pleasure. The bishop can exercise his authority over them at any time, but he hasn't yet. He entrusts pastoral care of the parish to the pastoral administrators and respects their decisions. Likewise, the pastoral administrators can go to the bishop with their pastoral problems or concerns, as can the priest-pastors."

"How would we get all this across to the parishioners?"

"The bishop insists on having a commissioning ceremony in the parish, much like a pastor's installation, in order to confirm that this person is the bishop's pastoral representative. The bishop is usually present. The letter of appointment is read aloud. The bishop expresses to the parish that this is his delegate, and the pastoral administrator swears the oath publicly. She or he then calls forth the priest who will be the sacramental minister. It offers a visual depiction of the lines of authority."

"How would Father Mueller fit in with a pastoral administrator here?"

"If Father Mueller is your sacramental minister, he'll preside at Sunday Masses and all the other sacraments. Most priests who do this try to affirm the pastoral administrator's authority. If folks ask them something, they refer them to the pastoral administrator. Their acceptance and support give the lay leader greater acceptance in the community. Often the pastoral administrator will consult the sacramental minister for help in decision making—especially if the priest respects the layperson as pastoral leader of the parish. It works best when they act as a pastoral team in providing leadership to the parish. But not all parishes are that lucky."

"Will people—especially the older people—really listen to

someone without a Roman collar?"

"There probably will be resistance at first; pastoral administrators have to earn the acceptance that a priest is given because of ordination. But the acceptance is great after a while. I think when lay leaders are competent and caring, positive, interested, and faith-filled, parishioners give them the authority they need. Most pastoral administrators are actually surprised at how much authority people give them. Having a good sense of the limits and extent of their own authority—negotiating authority inside—is really important. The people can tell when someone is not afraid of their own authority. Some parishioners who have difficulty with lay leaders have a poor sense of authority in themselves. Those who are healthy do fine. In general people have been very supportive and accepting of whatever gifts lay leaders bring. They appreciate them."

"Maybe this is prejudiced, but I just don't see how we could ever trust a layperson with our parish."

"Well, it may help to know that parishes that agree to receive lay leaders are involved throughout the interview and appointment process, and we try to prepare the parishioners. Lay leaders spend a year as pastoral associates in their parishes under the outgoing pastor. And the bishop trusts and values them. That's a pretty good start. You'll find that acceptance happens gradually. It's a growth experience for the community and the pastoral administrator. Lay parish leaders challenge everyone to imagine a church with a variety of authorities, including ourselves. They cause the whole Body of Christ to rise, like leaven."

"Hmm. I guess that's it for now. Thanks. I don't feel quite as worried about all this as I did before. You're coming to our next pastoral council meeting, right?"

"If I'm still welcome! I can also arrange for you to meet with a pastoral administrator who's already working in a parish in the diocese. Would that be helpful?"

"Very. I'll call you later in the week. Thanks again for coming."

"You're welcome! And, Mike, don't work too hard."

ぷ

A lot of Catholics feel like "Mike" and this typical pastoral council. They want to know what gives laypeople the right to lead parishes. They aren't ordained, so why should anyone listen to and follow them? These are questions about authority and obedience. Where does their authority come from and why should we do as they say?

A full answer to these questions requires a look at church law, the role of the bishop and priests of the diocese, diocesan practices, parish involvement in the process, and the personal authority of lay leaders themselves. It also requires an admission that obedience is just part of the ball game for Christians, whether Catholic or not, whether ordained or not. All Christians have to negotiate when to obey authority and when to claim their own authority as members of the baptized. Lay parish leaders can teach Catholics how to master this balancing act.

"By What Authority Are You Doing These Things?"

"By what authority are you doing these things? Who gave you this authority?" the high priests asked Jesus in the temple in Jerusalem (Mark 11:28; Matthew 21:23; Luke 20:2). They wanted to know and so do today's Catholics. By what authority can these ordinary Catholics lead parishes? Who authorizes them to do so?

These are valid questions that Catholics need answered before they can trust laypeople to lead their parishes. They bubble up not just from the spring of curiosity, but from the fears and uncertainty of those who ask, fears for the church, and uncertainty about their own personal authority. Like the high priests, who feared Jesus' influence with the people, wise Catholics know how easy it is for the church to be led astray—and this is uncharted territory.

They also know how easy it is to have their own authority stripped from them by a hierarchical system that can and does hand down decisions from the top, a system they expect lay leaders to perpetuate. It is not unreasonable, then, for pastoral councils to try to protect their own power and resist authoritarian diocesan decisions about the future of their parishes. Yes, they want to be assured that the people they will be expected to obey are properly authorized, but they also want and deserve to have a voice in choosing and "authorizing" those leaders. Questions about authority, then, often betray concerns about the questioner's own authority as much as they do about the authority of those in power.

So these seemingly straightforward questions regarding the authority of laypeople to lead parishes require some sophisticated answers. The first answer concerns the authorization that comes from above, from church law, from the local bishop, and from the priests of the diocese. Secondly, lay leaders must be given authority from below by the people they lead. And, ultimately, their authority rests deep within the lay leaders themselves, in the authority of baptism, an authorization that comes directly from Jesus, the highest of all authorities.

Authority from Above

Our starting point is authorization from above—from church law, the bishop, and the diocese—since questions of authority generally begin there and lower sources of authority find support from higher. To call this "higher authority" does not mean that it is the most important, most fundamental, or most trustworthy source. It is, instead, the issue at ground level that must be broken through before digging deeper into the soil to find the roots of Christian authority.

To begin with, no Christian congregation can call itself Catholic unless it is united in governance and ministry to the diocesan and universal Catholic Church. Even the words "parish" and "diocese," which both originally referred to a district of governance, suggest that the parish congregation is a small district of a larger district of the worldwide church. So the leader of every Catholic parish, whether ordained or lay, must be appointed by the bishop of the diocesan church in accord with universal church law. Without such authorization the person could still lead and the congregation would still be a church, but it would not, strictly speaking, be a Catholic parish. This makes the question of authorization from above especially significant for Catholic congregations.

Authorization from above is a complicated phenomenon that requires some detailed explanation. While it ordinarily comes with ordination, in the case of lay leaders authorization comes from church (or canon) law, delegation by the bishop, their title, commissioning ceremonies, diocesan policies, and clergy support. To explore these aspects of authorization we will turn to church documents and comments from lay parish leaders. The comments of the diocesan coordinators who were interviewed are particularly helpful in describing fruitful diocesan efforts to support the authority of lay parish leaders "from above."

Canon law. Official permission to appoint lay Catholics to lead parishes came in the 1983 *Code of Canon Law.* Canon (or church) law 517.2 reads:

> If, because of a lack of priests, the diocesan bishop has decided that participation in the exercise of the pastoral care of a parish is to be entrusted to a deacon, to another person who is not a priest, or to a community of persons, he is to appoint some priest who, provided with the powers and faculties of a pastor, is to direct the pastoral care.

Canon lawyer Father John A. Renken, who wrote the commentary on this canon in the *New Commentary on the Code of Canon Law,* points out several significant aspects of the law. First, the decision and appointments are to be made by the diocesan bishop alone. Second, the canon can only be implemented in the temporary and extraordinary situation of a real shortage of priests, again a judgment that the local bishop must make. Third, the priest who is appointed to direct the pastoral care "is not technically the pastor of the parish." Fourth, the nonpriest appointees "*participate* in pastoral care, but do not exercise the full care of souls, for such an office can be validly conferred only on a priest." Fifth, he recommends that dioceses develop "role descriptions" for all those who are appointed by this canon, since the canon itself is not specific about titles, obligations, or rights of the parties involved (Beal, 2000: 687–688, italics in the original). Each of these observations deserves a closer look.

Delegation by the bishop. Renken's first observation is that the local bishop has the authority to decide whether and when to appoint lay leaders in the diocese. He alone makes the appointment. This means that the source of a layperson's authority to lead a Catholic parish rests entirely in the bishop. Lay leaders do not serve under the priests who direct the pastoral care or the priests who celebrate sacraments with the parish.

Renken's second point is that each bishop evaluates the availability of priests and the proper courses of action in his own diocese. More than the actual number of parishes without priest-pastors in a given diocese, it is the bishop's point of view that accounts for the variation from diocese to diocese in the number of laypeople being appointed to lead parishes. Some bishops do not believe things have gotten *that bad.*

Renken's third point reinforces the lines of authority in this arrangement. The priest-director is not the pastor. Renken notes that in the 1977 draft of this canon the words "as the proper pastor of the parish" had described the priest appointee. However, the phrase was eliminated from the canon before it was approved "in order neither to restrict excessively the role of this nonpriest leadership figure nor to compress too much the scope of the competence of such a person" (Beal, 2000: 685).The appointed parish leader is given decision-making authority in the parish. The priest-director, often called canonical moderator, does not bear responsibility for parish decisions. He may direct, but it is the bishop who authorizes and oversees the pastoral care of the parish.

Title. In his fourth point Renken notes that nonpriests are not "pastors." They are appointed to *participate* in, not to 'take sole responsibility for, the pastoral care of parishes. They collaborate with the bishop and priests of the diocese in the exercise of the clergy's pastoral function. Even so, as their tasks are laid out in the next chapter it will become clear that these parish leaders may not "be" pastors in the sacramental sense or hold the office of pastor in the legal sense, but they certainly function as *de facto* pastors in parish life.

This discrepancy between their function and their office has made it difficult to settle on a fitting title for lay parish leaders, one that expresses both the intent of the law and the reality of their role in the parish. To complicate matters further, the previously cited *Instruction* on collaboration specifically prohibits many titles, such as " 'leader,' 'pastor,' 'chaplain,' 'coordinator,' 'moderator,' or other such similar titles which can confuse their role and that of the Pastor, who is always a Bishop or priest" (Practical Provisions, #1.3). The eleven lay leaders who were interviewed have six different titles—Parish Life Facilitator, Pastoral Leader, Pastoral Coordinator, Pastoral Administrator, Pastoral Director, and Parish Life Administrator. None feel that their title adequately describes their position or supports their authority. And most say that people commonly refer to them as lay pastors, without any confusion between their role and that of the priest.

The United States Conference of Catholic Bishops' Committee on Pastoral Practices has surveyed parish leaders who are not priests and is studying the question of titles but has not recommended a standard usage. In his commentary on canon 517.2, Dr. Renken suggests "parish life collaborator" since it reflects the theme of the *Instruction* (Beal, 2000: 686). Yet this term would meet frequent misinterpretation and require constant explanation. It would do little to clarify the role of lay parish leaders in the parish or to support their efforts to claim authority. Instead of searching for a title that describes their work, it may be more fruitful to find a title that reinforces the source of their authority.

The title "pastoral delegate" appropriately communicates their relationship with the local bishop and would likely provide support for leaders who are not priests. There are precedents for this title. Laypersons appointed to diocesan positions are sometimes named delegates rather than vicars. Laypersons have been named apostolic delegates to represent the bishop of Rome at international conferences and organizations. "Pastoral delegate" would be a good choice because it clarifies a parish leader's role and authority as the bishop's official pastoral representative to the parish. At the same time it is true to the intent of canon 517.2.

Commissioning. Dr. Renken's fifth observation recommends "role descriptions" to clarify and facilitate the functioning of this arrangement. One way that role description takes place is through commissioning rituals for parish leaders in their parishes. Eight of the lay parish leaders interviewed have had formal installation rituals similar to the one Sister Charlotte described to Mike. Both the lay leaders interviewed and their diocesan coordinators consider these rituals to be essential in communicating their authority as the bishop's official appointee. Here, as with titles, the rituals vary from diocese to diocese. Some dioceses are not yet commissioning lay parish leaders, but such rituals have been recommended by the United States bishops to express "the relationship of the bishop to the lay ecclesial minister" (Committee on the Laity, 1999: 42).

Diocesan policies. Since neither the priest-director nor the nonpriest appointee is legally or officially the pastor of the parish, dioceses have some freedom to describe areas of authority and accountability and develop policies that suit their particular situations, as Renken observes. This "role description" takes place largely through clear diocesan structures, job descriptions, guidelines for decision making, and training.

Sister Charlotte mentioned several of the ways in which the diocesan coordinators who were interviewed say dioceses seek to support the authority and functioning of lay parish leaders. Not all lay leaders interviewed feel the training and policies in their dioceses adequately support them. However, all the interviewees, even those who feel their own diocesan policies are inadequate, agree that clear diocesan structures, guidelines, and job descriptions are crucial in helping lay leaders claim accountability for their specific areas of authority and build working relationships with other diocesan pastoral leaders, particularly the clergy.

Three concise resources are currently available for dioceses. The Canon Law Society of America publishes "Pastoral Care in Parishes Without a Pastor," with practical suggestions on job descriptions and the selection process, a sample installation ceremony and contract. The National Pastoral Life Center published two center papers in 1995 on this ministry. "Pastoral Coordinators and Canon Law" focuses on the correct implementation of canon 517.2. "Pastoral Coordinators: Parish Leadership without a Resident Priest" summarizes pastoral experience. More will be said about the crucial role of diocesan policies in chapter 7.

Clergy support. Even without Roman collars to signify their authority, lay leaders can gain initial credibility in their parishes by their association with the clergy. This happens when the ordained publicly affirm the authority of lay leaders, thus throwing the mantle of office over their shoulders. While affirmation from nonordained diocesan coordinators also facilitates this process, the role of the clergy is key. Interviewees gave several examples of bishops and priest-directors, or canonical moderators, who affirm the role and authority of the lay leader in their contacts with parishioners. They also get significant support from sacramental ministers who remain in their roles and refer people with questions to the lay parish leaders.

One lay leader noted that perceived conflict between the sacramental minister and the lay leader can "polarize the parish" because the people do not know which authority figure to follow. Relationships between clergy and lay leaders will be discussed more fully later on. But it is significant to note here that clergy relationships with parishioners can provide invaluable support "from above" as lay leaders attempt to claim authority "from below."

Authority from Below

The lay leaders interviewed say that, while parishioners initially accepted their authority on the basis of the way the bishop and priests spoke about and interacted with them, their authority subsequently rested on their own ability to lead. Authorization from above may pave the way for authorization from below, but it cannot substitute for it.

Parish involvement. Involvement of the parish in the planning, decision-making, interview, appointment, and preparation processes is a vital means of creating authorization from below. Several of the lay leaders interviewed for this book believe their parishes were inadequately involved to prepare them to accept a lay leader. One diocesan coordinator described the sophisticated process they use to involve parishes at every step. It can serve as a pattern for dioceses seeking to involve parishes in the appointment of lay leaders.

In their diocese, long-range planning began with the diocesan pastoral council setting criteria for parish viability. A regional planning process involves parishes in preparing for the future. More than a year before a pastor's retirement, dialogue between the diocese and the parish pastoral council begins. Once a decision has been made to offer to appoint a lay leader in a parish, a diocesan representative of the bishop works with the parish staff and council in naming parishioners for a search committee. This committee identifies the qualities they are looking for in a parish leader and works with the diocesan personnel board in the interview process. The parish prays for discernment every Sunday.

When a candidate has been agreed upon, the diocesan representative supports the pastor in giving his approval. The lay leader is appointed to work in the parish with the outgoing pastor for a year before taking on parish leadership. At the end of this time, the parish has a farewell party for the outgoing pastor one Sunday and a welcome party for the lay leader the following Sunday.

Parish acceptance. All the factors mentioned are valuable in fostering parish acceptance of lay leaders. Yet even without adequate policies, planning, or support, lay parish leaders seem to be able to claim authority "from below" in their parishes. As early as a decade ago, when few dioceses had well-developed systems and policies, an attitudinal survey was conducted by the Institute for Pastoral Life. They surveyed lay parish leaders, diocesan personnel, and parishioners. *The*

Parish Life Coordinator: An Institute for Pastoral Life Study showed very high levels of parish acceptance in every area of parish life. Dr. Gary P. Burkart found that "Parishioners are overwhelmingly accepting of their PLCs" (Burkart, 1992: 136, 103). This suggests that another more significant factor supports their authority in the parish, and this is the authority that comes from within the lay leaders themselves.

Authority from Within

Both authorization from above and authorization from below support lay leaders as they develop a sense of inner authority to perform their appointed functions. Such support affirms and guides them when they find themselves in unfamiliar territory—and they do! But the reverse is also true. Without inner authority they would not be appointed to or keep their parish leadership positions. This authority "from within" is everything we said authority from above is not—the most important, most fundamental, and most trustworthy source of authority. It is primary in every sense: it comes first because it lies deep in the soil near the root of all Christian authority, Jesus Christ.

Inner authority manifests itself in the personal qualities of lay leaders. The lay leaders interviewed say that factors such as competence, self-confidence, and maturity convince bishops to entrust parishes to their care. Courage and perseverance, love and respect for others, a balance of self-possession and interdependence gradually convince parishioners to let go of resistance and trust their leadership. For the most part, these lay leaders do not need to be told or asked or authorized to act as they see fit because they find their authorization within themselves, in their baptismal sharing in the ministry of Christ.

It may now be obvious that considerable tension exists between whether lay parish leaders are effectively living out their ordinary baptismal vocation or participating extraordinarily and temporarily in a function properly belonging to priests. Those interviewed experience their authority as permanently rooted in their baptismal sharing in the ministry of Christ, not in a temporary sharing in the ministry of priests. However, the 1997 Vatican *Instruction* on collaboration emphasizes that lay parish leadership is a transitory, task-oriented, extraordinary sharing in the ministry of priests in response to an emergency situation. It is *not* a proper, permanent, ordinary exercise of the priesthood of the baptized (*Instruction*, Theological Principles, #2).

To clarify the issue we should separate the *position* of parish leaders from the *tasks* they perform. Certainly, the position of pastoral leader in a parish is always a delegated function and one ordinarily filled by a priest. As previously mentioned, no one, whether lay or ordained, can lead a Catholic parish without such authorization "from above." However, which of the specific tasks performed by lay parish leaders belong "properly" only to the distinct ministry of priests? For those significant tasks that do—and there are some—lay leaders admittedly need temporary authorization through the delega-tion of their bishop. But, as we will see in the next chapter, the majority of their work involves activities that these lay leaders *have done* before, any of the baptized *can do*, and many other lay ministers *are doing* in other settings without any authorization other than the inner authority of baptism.

Authority and Obedience

All these sources of authority—from above, from below, and from within—carry with them a responsibility for obedience. Parishioners are not the only Catholics who are expected to obey authorities. Both lay and ordained parish leaders are obliged to obey those who authorize them. To obey means literally to "hear and respond." Official leaders who do not "hear and respond" to the voice of their constituents soon lose their power because they no longer command the authority they need to get elected, much less to truly lead. Lay parish leaders, then, must hear and respond to the voice of their bishops, their coworkers, the people they serve, and the inner voice of the Spirit, otherwise they will lose both their authorization and their ability to lead Catholic parishes. It is a difficult balancing act. Jesus and Paul can again serve as role models for their skill at balancing authority and obedience.

Jesus. In the temple of Jerusalem, Jesus ignored the outrage of both the crowd and the Jewish authorities when he overturned the money-changers' tables (Mark 11:15–17). Here he heard and responded to the inner authority of the Spirit and resisted external authorities. Yet he obeyed the authentic external authority of his mother at the wedding feast at Cana (John 2:1–11). And this same Jesus, who had full authority to command his fate, was "obedient to the point of death—even death on a cross" (Philippians 2:8).

Does this mean that Jesus relinquished his own inner authority and gave in to external authority on the cross? No. John's gospel says that he laid down his life of his own accord (John 10:18). The Eucharistic Prayer of the Catholic liturgy says something similar. It calls Jesus' death "a death he freely accepted." In other words, Jesus chose to bow to an unjust external authority in obedience to his own inner authority. Jesus always heard and responded to the inner voice of the Spirit; sometimes this meant obeying and sometimes it meant resisting external authority.

Paul. Paul also obeyed his own inner authority. His response to the Spirit in baptism was immediate and unequivocal. He gave up all his former authority "from above" as a Pharisee (Philippians 3:5) in order to obey the voice of the Spirit within that sent him as an apostle to the gentiles. He did not wait for the Twelve to authorize him. He had his authorization from "the Lord" (1 Corinthians 9:1, 2). His bold letters to the churches demonstrate that he was not afraid to challenge those who authorized him "from below." At his meeting in Jerusalem with James and Peter, when he championed the freedom of gentile Christians as equals of Jewish Christians, Paul showed that he was not afraid to challenge "higher" authorities either. However, he also witnessed his conviction that the authorization of those authentic authorities was worth fighting for (Galatians 2:1–14).

And yet Paul willingly gave up his own freedom and taught his churches to do the same when the Spirit told him it was for the common good. He made himself a "slave" to the needs of others, thus obeying the external authority of the community, the Body of Christ

(1 Corinthians 9:19). Like Jesus, Paul always obeyed his inner authority—a voice that guided him at times to fight for freedom and at other times to become a slave to the needs of the church.

Lay parish leaders are constantly challenged to balance the voices of authority that have claims on them. Like Paul, they sometimes must relinquish their own inner freedom and obey external authority when the Spirit tells them it is for the common good of the Body of Christ. Their example shows all Catholics how to embrace both the authority and the obedience that flow from Christian baptism.

The Authority of All the Baptized

Perhaps now we should ask the authority questions again: "By what authority are you doing these things? Who gave you this authority?" How do ordinary Catholics become authorized to minister in the name of Jesus? Not surprisingly, the experience of lay parish leaders suggests that baptism is the fundamental source of the authority of all Christians.

In baptism Jesus authorizes them to be more than simply his disciples, or followers. He sends them out as his apostles. An apostle is one who is sent forth on a mission. Canon law 216 confirms that "Since they participate in the mission of the Church, all the Christian faithful have the right to promote or sustain apostolic action by their own undertakings" (Beal, 2000: 271). In baptism Christians are sent forth as "genuine apostles" to continue Christ's mission in the world (*Decree on the Apostolate of the Laity*, #13). No one needs to wait for Father's invitation or permission. The Spirit authorizes them from within. The next chapter will examine how Catholics can exercise their "apostolic" authority.

Yet the Spirit's voice does not only come from within. The Spirit also speaks through the church in the external authorities of the hierarchy (from above) and the community (from below). Those authorities also call Catholics to obey—and it is indeed a balancing act. One person may question the church's teachings on abortion while another questions the teachings on the death penalty. One may struggle with the expectation to reach out to the "undesirables" whom Christians tend to exclude, while another struggles with the expectation to join the community at Mass every Sunday. One parish may resist a diocesan decision to close their parish while another resists "obeying" a lay leader. Even the inner voice of the Spirit is not always easy to obey, much less understand or hear clearly. Balancing which voice to hear and respond to can be tricky business.

Mature adulthood involves the ability to discern and claim one's inner authority while at the same time maintaining a healthy relationship with external authority. It takes courage to resist pressure from external authorities whom one judges to be wrong. It takes humility to "freely accept" the authentic authority of others even when it causes one to suffer. Yes, baptized Catholics have the authority to act as Jesus' apostles; yet they are also slaves to one another, as Paul was, for the common good. As with Mike's pastoral council, listening and responding to the voice of the Spirit requires that Catholics take the time and effort to dialogue with all the authorities—above, below, and within—that have a legitimate claim on them. Baptism authorizes all the baptized to continue Christ's apostolic mission, yet binds them to "obey"—to hear and respond to—one another in love.

Questions to Consider

- Which form of authorization do you think is most valuable for lay parish leaders and why?
- What title would you give to lay leaders of Catholic parishes?
- What should a pastoral council do if they disagree with a diocesan proposal for their parish?
- What would help your parish to accept a lay leader?
- Give examples of possible conflicts between a lay leader's inner voice and the hierarchy, between the hierarchy and the community, or between the community and the lay leader. In those examples, which of the three "authorities" should the lay leader obey?

- What does it feel like to think of yourself as a "genuine apostle?"
- When is it difficult for you to hear and respond to the Spirit within? What do you do in those cases?
- How do you balance claiming and obeying authority in your faith life?

∽ CHAPTER 4 ∽

What Can They Do?
Priestly Service

*M*ike had just looked at the clock a third time when the pastoral administrator at Holy Name and St. Raphael's parishes walked in the door.

"Hi! You must be Mike Lopez. I'm Stephen Dvorak. Sorry to be late. A sick parishioner took a turn for the worse and the family wanted me there."

"Don't worry about it. The maintenance guy told me what was going on and I had some time to spare today. It's good to meet you. How's the patient?"

"Oh, Eleanor won't be with us much longer, but she's had a long life and says she 'can't wait to go home.' She's quite a source of inspiration. Let's talk in our luxurious all-purpose meeting room here. I understand you're the parish council president at Saints Perpetua and Felicity and you folks have been asked to consider getting a pastoral administrator."

"Yup. Thanks for letting me come and talk to you about your work."

"Happy to do it. It's really a wonderful ministry. The people are life giving. I get to walk with them through the events of their lives— sacraments, dying, illness. Being present—that's what it's all about."

"I guess that's mostly what I was wondering. What exactly do you do? Like, with Eleanor, you anointed her?"

"No. I don't do sacraments because I'm not ordained; but I can do other things besides anoint. I listen and pray with them. I tell them, 'These are the prayers that Father Tom would say if he were here.' I use the same book. I bring them communion. I just try to do my best to minister to their spiritual needs."

"What if a priest doesn't make it in time?"

"To anoint them before they die? I do a lot of education about anointing, not as an emergency, but as a health-care sacrament. We have it regularly at the nursing home every three months. When someone's very ill and wants to be anointed, I do everything I can to get a priest there. If there's no one but me available I provide the best pastoral care I can for them. Sometimes I help them see the situation differently, re-vision their needs. In general, people's needs are getting met, but sometimes not in the way they would like. People want priests and can't always have them. I grieve for them. I feel sorry that they can't have the care they would prefer, but I'm glad I can at least give them trained care."

"And people are okay with that?"

"Some people think that without a Roman collar, what I do doesn't count. The newcomers are the ones who insist that I call a priest. Once, one of the parishioners went around me to a neighboring priest. But most people are very appreciative. I find that God does minister through me even when sacraments aren't available. Community is primary for them and I'm their link to the parish community. Last week I took the Eucharist to a prisoner in solitary confinement. Each of us was fed, and the guards were watching us. I came home and cried. The next morning I started crying again. I think 'sacraments' happen on all different levels. I'm Eucharist for others and they're Eucharist for me."

"It sounds like you make a big difference in people's lives."

"Most of the difference I make is in one-on-one pastoral visits. Visiting shut-ins is only part of it. It really is a ministry of presence. Even though I've been in ministry before, I don't know if presence has been so important. Here it's the main thing. Even having a cup of coffee with someone is part of my job. Just being available and accessible, being with people whether it's a major event or day-to-day life. And you don't have to be ordained to do that. I've had people who 'confess' to me. And that's fine with me. The tradition of lay confession is common and old. You can't stop people when they're ready. You have to be there for them and listen to them. I'm the listener."

"What else do you do?"

"Everything a priest-pastor would do except preside at sacraments. Pastoral care and administration of Holy Name and St. Raphael's parishes. I nurture and guide the pastoral and finance councils. I've done lots of staff and ministry formation. I work with the worship committee on liturgical seasons and rites. That's important because Sunday liturgy is when people are here. I preside at wakes and communion services and train others in the parish to lead prayer and visit the sick. Occasionally, I preach on Sundays. I help prepare couples for marriage, families for baptisms and funerals, offer spiritual formation and Bible study, and I'm part of the team that does initiation ministry. I organize parish life—coordinate people's gifts and talents, facilitate social outreach, evangelization, religious education and ecumenical ministries, keep order, foster community life. Plus the administrative tasks—communication, mail, finances, keeping records, connecting with the diocese, plant management, long-range planning, making decisions now and then."

"Do you ever get to go home?"

"Well, I delegate a lot. Most important is to be the gatherer, the focal point. I'm the person who calls, initiates, invites people to participate in the parish. It's a question of providing a pastoral presence. Someone who's with them in the community. With me living in the rectory they feel they have someone who's interested in them as people. They haven't been fed the way that I can feed them for years. They say, 'You bring the church to me.' "

"What do they call you?"

"Mostly they call me Stephen. Sometimes they'll introduce me as the lay pastor. The chancery doesn't like it, but that's the reality of the work I'm doing. I think people want to designate you for the kind of service you're giving to them. There are many faces to

pastoring. I don't think that only priests 'pastor.' In people's experience, folks other than priests do that."

"So, when do you start saying Mass?"

"Very funny. I actually think it's okay that I'm not ordained.
Since I've been doing this I've come to realize how much laypeople
can do in the Catholic Church. It's getting people used to other
people leading worship, taking communion, taking responsibility.
When parishioners see that as a layperson I can shepherd a
community, I think it challenges them to become more Christian, to
take on more shepherding in their own lives, to become Christian
leaders."

"I guess I'd better watch out if we get a pastoral administrator.
Thanks, Stephen. You gave me a lot to think about."

"You're more than welcome, Mike. Let me know how things
turn out."

⌁

*C*anon 517.2 calls the function of lay parish leaders "participation
in the exercise of the pastoral care of a parish." In the description
given here by the character "Stephen," we can see precisely what this
entails. The lay leaders interviewed take responsibility for all the
pastoral and administrative activities of the parish. A few of these
activities ordinarily would be performed by the ordained, but most
are among the ordinary responsibilities of baptized Catholics.

While some fear that this ministry will obscure the distinct
identity of the priesthood of the ordained, instead it is revealing the
identity of the baptized. The ministry of lay parish leaders is stripping
away layers of clericalism that have obscured the common priesthood
of the baptized for centuries. What does the priesthood of the
baptized look like? What activities are proper to the members of this
common priesthood? Like "Mike," many Catholics don't know, and
might not want to know, the full extent of the secular, missionary
priesthood that they hold in common. Reflected in the work of lay
parish leaders, the baptized can clearly see the priestly image and
ministry of Christ into which all Catholics are baptized.

The Activities of Lay Parish Leaders

Stephen's remarks reveal what the life of a typical lay parish leader consists of. Over and over again, those who were interviewed described the comprehensive nature of their work in the parish by saying they do everything a priest-pastor would do except the sacraments. This includes coordinating community life, facilitating liturgical participation, forming parishioners, guiding the work of councils and committees, and managing parish administration. In short, they guide and nurture the ministry of Christ in the parish. Like priest-pastors they take responsibility for all the activities and decisions in the parish but, unlike priest-pastors, they do not preside at sacraments. Above all, they say that their most important function is to provide a pastoral presence in the parish. Gradually, parishioners come to claim that these lay leaders represent their parish communities and the life of faith they share.

Community. The ministry of the early Christian community is summarized in the Acts of the Apostles (Acts 2:42–47). This ministry includes four areas of activity, one of which is *koinonia*, or community life. The lay parish leaders interviewed spend a good deal of time building a spirit of mutual love and solidarity in their parishes. One described herself as "the gatherer—the one who calls, initiates, invites, and delegates." Another emphasized his efforts to name and thank parishioners publicly. Others spoke of greeting and talking with parishioners on Sundays to foster a spirit of hospitality. One highlighted the bulletin as a prime resource for knitting the community together. Lay leaders coordinate parish life, facilitating efforts of parishioners to get to know and care for one another. They see themselves as a pivot around which community life revolves. Lay leaders conscientiously create opportunities for the parishes they lead to become more closely united as the Body of Christ.

Liturgy. A second core area of activity in the early church is *leitourgia*, or prayer and worship. All of the lay leaders interviewed lead prayer services in the parishes—informal prayer at committee meetings, liturgies of the word, word and communion services, wakes, and stations of the cross, to name a few. They schedule and orchestrate masses for Sundays and holy days. They prepare specific rites for seasons, initiation, and other sacraments. They arrange for priests to preside at Eucharist, other sacraments, and funerals. A few have performed emergency baptisms. About half of those interviewed preach occasionally at Sunday masses or lead "Sunday Celebrations in the Absence of a Priest" with some regularity. Some lay leaders vest and take visible roles at Mass on Sundays, but many prefer to remain in the assembly with the other parishioners.

Lay parish leaders also pray with parishioners in home and institutional visits. They use spontaneous prayer as well as scriptural, ritual, and familiar devotional prayers. Often they will pray the ritual for taking Holy Communion to the sick. One lay leader regularly provides resources for home prayer to all parishioners. Those interviewed also encourage parishioners to take on liturgical leadership. They guide the work of parish liturgy committees and those who care for the environment for worship. Most encourage and form others to lead the parish in ritual prayer, to do most liturgical preparations, and to take communion to the sick.

Formation. The Acts of the Apostles also speaks of the church's ministry of *didache*, or teaching. A commitment to spiritual formation in the parish is common to the lay parish leaders who were interviewed. Several described this work as "feeding" the parishioners. The lay leaders train people for various ministries within and outside the parish. They invest time in forming parish councils and committees. They participate in parish scripture study, religious education, and sacramental preparation ministries. They also encourage parishioners to join faith-sharing groups and attend formation sessions available in their dioceses. The lay leaders interviewed seem to use every method available to them to nurture the faith of parishioners and help them to teach one another the ramifications of belonging to the people of God.

Ministry. The fourth fundamental area of life in the early Christian community was *diaconia*, or the ministry of service. Lay leaders interviewed say that they "animate" and "guide" the various ministries in their parish. They seek to enable others to serve rather than doing all the ministries themselves. We have already mentioned their support for the communal, liturgical, and formational ministries of the parish. The specific ministries of service, or outreach, also require their attention. These ministries vary from parish to parish depending on the needs of the community in which the parish is situated and the particular gifts of the parishioners. One of the interviewees spoke of prison ministry, another of ecumenical outreach, another of their soup kitchen and homeless shelter, another of the food and clothing bank they operate jointly with the other religious congregations in town. Every lay leader interviewed is involved in supporting the parish in its ministry of service.

Administration. None of the four areas of the "spiritual" life of the church mentioned can proceed if practical "worldly" matters—decisions, communication, finances, records, plant and personnel management—are ignored. Lay leaders are responsible for the administration of their parishes. Since some of the parishes are tiny, many lay leaders do everything from writing checks to writing the bulletin, from keeping the bathrooms clean to keeping the books clean. Others with larger communities oversee the work of parishioners and staff members. Those lay leaders find themselves most involved in managing personnel and parish communication. Most of those interviewed have pastoral and finance councils with whom they share decision making. Yet, as in every Catholic parish, these councils are consultative. The lay leaders, like pastors, have ultimate responsibility for parish decisions and the income and outflow of parish funds.

Pastoral presence. In the conversation at the beginning of this chapter, Stephen reiterated what lay parish leaders say is the most significant aspect of their ministry—providing a "pastoral presence." Even the Vatican *Instruction* on collaboration describes their function as "pastoral care" (Practical Provisions, #4.1). Those interviewed emphasize the importance of their living in homes in the community (sometimes the rectory) and being physically as well as emotionally available to parishioners.

In the past, some of the parishes they serve have had nonresident priest-pastors who could only be physically present on Sundays. Other parishes have experience with priest-pastors who were physically present but were unable to make themselves emotionally available to their parishioners for reasons such as busyness, advanced age, emotional ill health, or a hierarchical understanding of their relationship with the parish. The lay leaders interviewed place high priority on personal interaction with parishioners, spending time with them and listening to the stories of their everyday lives.

Community representative. As time goes by, parishioners come to see a lay parish leader as representing their parish community. In visits to the sick, in diocesan affairs, in neighborhood events, the lay leaders interviewed gradually were perceived as representing the Catholic communities that they lead. They say this process facilitates their ministry. It gives them greater credibility and adds effectiveness to their words and deeds. They become effective signs of the ministry of Christ present in their parishes. Since Catholics say that sacraments are "effective signs" of Christ's active presence in the world, the ministry of lay leaders can be said to carry "sacramentally" the presence of Christ that abides and works in their parishes. Their ministry takes on a sacramental quality, signifying the Body of Christ really present in the Christian communities they lead.

Activities Proper to the Ordained

Under ordinary circumstances, which of the tasks of lay parish leaders would be reserved exclusively to priests? In the language of church documents the question would be, "Which entail an 'extraordinary exercise' of functions proper to the ministerial priesthood?" There are some. A tiny minority of lay leaders have permission to preside regularly at baptisms and marriages. These fit in the category of tasks that laypersons cannot ordinarily do. All lay parish leaders, however, participate in the governance of their parishes. This is an "extraordinary" sharing in a function "ordinarily" reserved to priests.

In the *Dogmatic Constitution on the Church* (#28), the bishops of the Second Vatican Council describe the office of "presbyter" (as priests are properly called) and its distinct sharing in the priestly, prophetic, and pastoral ministry of Christ. A comparison of the activities of lay leaders to these three specific duties of priests reveals what is extraordinary about the work of lay parish leaders. It is not that they perform tasks that laypeople ordinarily cannot do. It is their position of pastoral responsibility for all that happens in and through the parish.

Priestly. The priestly function of priests is to lead a holy life, to pray for the church, to foster the active participation of the community in the liturgy, and to preside over the community's sacraments—"primarily the Eucharist" (*Lumen gentium*, #28; Canon 528.2). All of the baptized are also called to "lead a holy life and promote the growth of the Church and its continual sanctification" (Canon 210). And lay liturgists and liturgy committees commonly take responsibility for fostering liturgical participation in American parishes.

This leaves the question of whether lay parish leaders preside at sacraments. Most do not. The prayer services which laypersons lead might be described as "sacramental"—effective signs of the ministry of Christ in and through the community—but they are not among the church's seven "sacraments" *per se*. As a result, presiders at these liturgical services do not need to be ordained (Canon 230.3).

Do lay leaders say Mass? No. Do they preside at the sacrament of reconciliation or anointing? No. Some interviewees said that parishioners have confessed their sins to them in the course of spiritual counseling, but this is not a sacrament. The sacrament of reconciliation requires absolution by a priest. Similarly, a layperson cannot administer the sacrament of the sick. Instead, in their ministry to the dying, most of those interviewed bring communion and pray the prayers for the sick, something any baptized person can do (Canons 910.2; 911.2).

Infrequently lay parish leaders preside at baptisms, marriages, and funerals. A lay leader may baptize someone who is in danger of death, but this is not extraordinary. Hospital staff and chaplains are often called upon to baptize. It is among the responsibilities of all Christians to baptize in emergency situations (Canon 861.2). In the absence of clergy, laypeople may preside at noneucharistic funeral liturgies, even though funerals are an activity "especially entrusted to the pastor" (Canon 530). In a very few Catholic dioceses in the United States, the bishops have granted permission for laypersons to baptize regularly and to witness Catholic marriages, which is allowed by Canon 1112.

Prophetic. As ministers of the word, priest-pastors have a responsibility to preach a homily on Sundays and holy days, interpreting Christian life by the light of the Word and the Eucharist. They are also responsible for fostering justice, for teaching the faith of the church, especially to the young, and for spreading the Gospel beyond the members of the parish (Canon 528.1).

All these tasks, except the homily, are functions that laypeople, including lay parish leaders, also ordinarily perform. Canon 785.1 says that qualified laypersons can serve in the role of "catechist," or teacher. Laypersons now teach and direct religious education, evangelization, and sacramental formation in most American Catholic parishes. Beyond that, all the baptized are to "work so that the divine message of salvation more and more reaches all people" (Canon 211).

Regarding the Sunday homily, the *Instruction* on collaboration clearly delineates that it is the sole responsibility of the ordained. Yet "laypersons can be permitted to preach . . . if necessity requires it in certain circumstances or it seems advantageous in particular cases" (Canon 766). In some dioceses, lay parish leaders are not permitted to preach on Sundays. In others, they preach at Sunday services with some regularity. A small majority of the lay leaders interviewed say they preach on Sundays. They preach when there is not a priest available for Sunday Mass or when the lay leader's preaching would be fruitful for the community. In his commentary, Rev. James A. Coriden notes that this canon "does not view lay preaching as a substitute for clerical ministry" nor as an "extraordinary" ministry for laypersons. Preaching, too, "is a fully legitimate lay function" (Beal, 2000: 927).

Pastoral. The pastoral functions of priests include pastoral care, spiritual guidance, and governance of the diocesan church in collaboration with the bishop and other priests. A priest who is named pastor exercises "the pastoral care of the community entrusted to him under the authority of the diocesan bishop in whose ministry of Christ he has been called to share" (Canon 519). Pastoral care requires a pastor to "visit families, sharing especially in the cares, anxieties, and griefs of the faithful, strengthening . . . and prudently correcting them . . . help the sick . . . seek out the poor . . . and foster . . . Christian life in the family" (Canon 529.1).

These responsibilities are ordinarily shared with all the baptized. As Stephen pointed out, lay leaders coordinate pastoral visits and arrange for people's spiritual and sacramental needs to be met. It is common in large parishes for lay pastoral associates or pastoral ministers to fulfill these same functions. According to *Lumen gentium* (#28), however, the "supreme" means through which priest-pastors exercise pastoral care is through presiding at the Sunday Eucharist, where Christ spiritually guides and nourishes the community at the Lord's table. Of course, laypersons never preside at the church's Eucharist.

Governance over parish decisions and financial matters is the source and sign of a pastor's power in parish life. Although a parish pastor is only sharing in the bishop's function as shepherd (pastor) of the diocese, ordinarily in a Catholic parish the buck stops at the priest-pastor. "He is to take care that the goods of the parish are administered according to the norm of law" (Canon 532). He has the power to direct the life and finances of the community as he sees fit.

Lay leaders participate extraordinarily in parish governance through their responsibility for parish finances and decisions about parish life. Here lies the key difference between the function of lay parish leaders and the ordinary responsibilities of all the baptized. It is not about what laypeople can and can't do. Any qualified layperson can perform most of the activities of lay parish leaders. All the baptized have the "right and even at times the duty" to contribute to parish decision-making processes "according to the knowledge, competence, and prestige which they possess" (Canon 212.3).

What is extraordinary about lay parish leaders is that they are temporarily delegated the position and power of pastors, albeit without pastors' sacramental character, abilities, title, or office. It is not the *activities* of lay parish leaders that are extraordinary, but their *position* and their *power* in the life of the parishes they lead. No one should be surprised, then, if some of the ordained who hold positions of power in the Catholic Church demonstrate fear of sharing that power with lay parish leaders. Both their sharing in power and the clergy's willingness to share power in this ministry can be seen as truly "extraordinary."

Is their sharing in pastoral care and governance confusing Catholics about the difference between the ordained and the laity? On the contrary, as lay ecclesial ministers of all kinds have become commonplace in parish life, American Catholics have recognized that pastoral leadership comes from a variety of persons besides priests. This recognition does not confuse; it clarifies the identity and activities that belong "properly" and "ordinarily" to the common priesthood of all the baptized. It is breaking down the simplistic notion that *only* the ordained can be "pastors" while the laity can *only* be sheep.

The Priesthood of All the Baptized

The whole Christian community is responsible for the ministry of Christ through community life, prayer and worship, teaching and spreading the Good News, and the ministry of service. And most of the activities of lay parish leaders are tasks that laypeople can and should undertake. They flow from the common priesthood in which *all* the baptized participate. What characterizes this "common priesthood of the baptized"? It is a common, secular, missionary sharing in the priesthood of Christ.

Common. To say that the priesthood of the baptized is "common" does not mean that it is ordinary, unrefined, or worthless in comparison to an ordained priesthood that is extraordinary, refined, and precious. The common character of the baptismal priesthood testifies that this priesthood is what all Christians hold "in common." It binds together *all* of the baptized—the ordained and the nonordained—in the one priestly identity and ministry of Christ. It is the root of every Christian's vocation, gifts, authority, and responsibilities. No one person has to do everything; but *all* are bound to exercise the priesthood of Christ, which they share in common.

Secular—and sacred. The priesthood of the baptized is said to have a "secular" character. If we remember that Christ's mission itself has this secular character, we can better understand why the baptismal priesthood is primarily secular. Christ lived in and ministered to the world. The place and purpose of the church is to continue Christ's ministry in and to the world. In chapter two we noted that every ministry within the church fosters Christ's ministry to the world. Yet it has often been thought that there were two distinct realms: The sacred, or holy, was the place of sacraments, chapels, prayer, peace, solitude, and *the ordained*; the secular, or worldly, was the place of financial planning, hospitals, soccer games, conflict, family relationships, and *the laity*.

Such an interpretation is no longer defensible. In the *Pastoral Constitution on the Church in the Modern World*, the bishops of Vatican II placed the sacred ministry of *all* the baptized squarely within the world where it belongs. Laypeople are not worldly while the ordained are otherworldly; *all* the baptized are to live holy lives *within* the world of family relationships and human activity. The church is not a sacred place from which to withdraw from the "unsacred" world; it is a privileged place from which to view the world with new eyes and recognize and foster the sacredness there. There are no unsacred people, places, or activities, only uncultivated sacredness.

The ordained may focus their attention primarily inward, on shepherding the ministry of the church. The laity may focus primarily outward, on exercising this ministry in the world of family and work. As Pope John Paul II said in 1985 after the bishops' synod on the laity: "The 'world' thus becomes the place and the means for the lay faithful to fulfill their Christian vocation" (*CL*, #15, p.36). The sacred/secular distinction helps to clarify the right and obligation of the *ordained* to govern activities that happen under the "sacred" auspices of the Catholic Church. It highlights the right and obligation of the *laity* to undertake activities to transform the "secular" world without oversight from the ordained.

Yet this distinction can easily obscure the priesthood that all the baptized hold in common—a priesthood that seeks to bridge the gap between the sacred and the secular. The Holy One who entered into human flesh in order to transform the world does not allow the ordained or the laity to separate the two "worlds" or to relinquish responsibility for either. The ministry of *all* the baptized must simultaneously foster the "sanctification" of the church and "consecrate"—or make sacred—the secular world (*LG*, #33, 34).

Missionary. In the last chapter, I emphasized the apostolic sending that authorizes the baptized to continue the mission of Christ. *All* the baptized, ordained and nonordained, participate in the sanctifying, teaching, and guiding mission of the church in the world. "Made sharers in their own way in the priestly, prophetic, and royal function, they [all the baptized] are called to exercise the mission which God has entrusted to the church to fulfill in the world, in accord with the condition proper to each" (Canon 204.1, Beal, 2000: 245). In other words, all Catholics are sent forth to continue Christ's messianic— that is, priestly, prophetic, and pastoral—mission in the world.

This messianic mission has priestly elements such as leading others in prayer; praying for, naming, and cultivating the sacredness of the world; and seeking personal holiness. It has prophetic elements such as teaching others the faith of the church, welcoming strangers, listening with compassion, unmasking deception, challenging oppression, and sharing the good news of the liberation that Jesus has brought—and still seeks to bring—into the world. It has pastoral elements, such as guiding the life of the Christian community, caring for the earth, reconciling hurts, feeding the hungry, clothing the naked, and reforming unjust systems until they serve the "least" members of Christ's family (Matthew 25:31–46). Whether in professional church leadership, in volunteer ministries, in family life and relationships, in their work, or in society, all Catholics—both lay and ordained—are responsible to participate in Christ's mission to God's beloved world.

Priesthood. In a recent pastoral letter on ministry, *As I Have Done For You*, Cardinal Roger Mahoney of Los Angeles writes that "all the baptized faithful share in the one priesthood of Jesus Christ" (*Origins*, May 4, 2000: 744). Cardinal Mahoney calls on both priests and laity to recall the words of Jesus to his disciples after washing their feet and recognize that, in these words, Christ "urges us, one and all: 'As I have done for you, you should do also' (John 13:15)" (*Origins*, May 4, 2000: 747). He reminds *all* Catholics that theirs is a sacrificial priesthood of service, which they embrace anew each time they celebrate the Eucharist:

> The Christian community is formed in and through the eucharist (1 Corinthians 10:16–17). It becomes the body of Christ, who is priest, and it joins itself to Christ the priest in his return to the Father in his self-offering, thereby becoming a priestly community endowed with the flourishing of gifts to sanctify and evangelize the world (1 Peter 2:9) (*Origins*, May 4, 2000: 748).

Priesthood, whether "common" or ordained, has nothing to do with power or position. It is through lives of service and sacrifice that *all* the baptized are to extend Christ's priestly mission and make God's world a holy place.

The common priesthood of the baptized is anything but common. All hold in common their participation in the secular, missionary priesthood of Jesus Christ. Sent forth from the Eucharist to make Christ's priestly, prophetic, and pastoral presence effective in the world, *all* the baptized seek to bridge the gap between the sacred and the secular by their lives of service. They can only do so if they remain united to one another and to the source of their uncommon priesthood, Jesus Christ.

As Stephen said in the opening conversation of this chapter, one "does not have to be ordained" to engage in priestly tasks. And what the baptized do *does* "count." Even without a Roman collar, "Christ does minister through" the baptized. The priestly activity of all the baptized, like that of lay parish leaders, is "sacramental" in the broad sense of the word: It is an effective sign of Christ's sacrificial service on behalf of the world.

Pope John Paul II, in his apostolic letter for the closing of the Jubilee Year, *"Novo Millennio Ineunte,"* proposed that "the church of the third millennium will need to encourage all the baptized and confirmed to be aware of their active responsibility in the church's life" (*NMI* #46). To "encourage" Catholics to take up their priestly responsibilities is to empower the common priesthood of all the baptized. Ultimately, it is to foster the priestly ministry of Christ in the world. This is exactly what lay parish leaders are doing, and it will be the topic of the next chapter.

Questions to Consider

- Who in your parish performs the various activities discussed in this chapter? What does the pastor do?
- What surprises you about the activities proper to priest-pastors? What bothers you?
- How might having a lay leader affect your parish's relationship with the clergy?
- Is there more that joins or more that divides lay and ordained Catholics? Explain.
- In what ways are Catholics tempted to separate the sacred from the secular? How is this problematic?
- How do you cultivate the sacredness of the world in which you live?
- Which priestly, prophetic, or pastoral activities have you engaged in? Which might you try?
- Which characteristic of the priesthood of the baptized—common, secular, missionary, or priestly—do you resonate with most? Why?

∽ CHAPTER 5 ∽

How Does It Work?
Leadership Among Equals

*T*wo, please. Nonsmoking."

"Nice place, Denise. I haven't been here before."

"Just a neighborhood hangout. The owners are from our parish. I wasn't sure I'd get to the pastoral administrators' meeting today, Stephen; but I'm glad I did."

"Me, too. I always get something out of it—share experiences, challenge each other, learn a few things. I'm beginning to develop some strong friendships in that group, too. How long have you been pastoral administrator at Saints Perpetua and Felicity, six months or so?"

"It'll be a year at the end of the summer. Feels like a lifetime. Rhubarb pie, please."

"I'll have the same. What's the parish like?"

"We have four-hundred-some households, 90 percent Latino. The old Italian community is dwindling. Some people call this the ghetto. It feels like home to me. Tell me about yours."

"Since Holy Name is only an hour from the city, we're kind of divided now between wealthier city folks who commute to work and poorer rural old-timers. There are 180 registered households. The second church, St. Raphael's, has only twenty-eight families. It's farther out. Are things going all right for you in the 'ghetto'?"

"I guess. I knew there'd be some resistance and rejection, but I didn't realize how stressful it would be. These folks have perceptions of what married women are supposed to do and I think I caught them off guard. It's especially difficult with the Latino men. Two families have decided not to be involved since I came—they go to the neighboring parish that has a priest-pastor."

"Don't take it personally. I'm not sure it's any better for me, a single man who's not a priest. They don't know what to think of me. I had a little bit of negativity from a family that grew up on a farm near Holy Name when I came. They couldn't accept my role and authority, my veto right on the council. They resented my leadership, so they left."

"I'm glad I'm not the only one! I get so wrapped up in things. The biggest challenge for me is setting boundaries. I truly love these people, but this ministry can eat up your whole life. The parishioners almost expect me to be that way and I have to be the one who steps back."

"That's an ongoing struggle for me, too, especially living at the old rectory, but at least I have some control over it. Right now I'm more discouraged about diocesan politics. Maintaining hope and optimism in the face of clericalist attitudes is tough for me."

"I think I'm too busy in the parish to really understand all that yet. Although Father Mueller and I have a great relationship. He's a mentor to me. I try to emulate him in my ministry."

"Wonderful. I needed to hear some good news. As far as my parishes go, St. Raphael's had a part-time pastoral administrator before me, and they've always been very receptive; but with the folks at Holy Name I had to start from scratch, like you're doing. It took them about a year to stop asking where Father was, but they're coming around. Some of those who fought me the hardest are now my biggest supporters."

"I hope I can say the same soon. I had some trouble with one member of the finance council arguing with me about money. My salary was higher than he wanted to pay. I got together the records on all the benefits the parish priest had received. The rest of the finance council supported me and that took care of the issue."

"Nice job, Denise."

"That's the exception, though. Most people appreciate my leadership. When the bishop appointed me, some people were just glad he didn't close the parish. Others were happy for my competence, energy, and hard work, which they saw right away. Now most of them are proud of me. I was a breath of life here."

"At my parishes they're overjoyed to have someone there to call and rely on. Because I'm there, they feel they have an active community. Actually, the parishes are thriving."

"I'm experiencing the same thing. What do you think that's about?"

"Well, I'm a layperson. People don't see me as very different from themselves. They're not sure the priests understand them. I know what they're going through. I connect with them on their terms. They say that I talk about religious experience in language they can understand. I think my lay status is both a gift and a challenge for them."

"I sense that, too. Maybe I'm more accessible personally than a priest, perhaps as a woman or as a layperson. When I preach, I bring in my family experience and might have more rapport with the lived experience of the parishioners. In marriage preparation we share our struggles—this has been a grace for me and for the parish. It really feels like an equal exchange to me."

"Yes, and people know everyone is equal in my mind. I came in and tried to listen to people. I invited people in, to be a part. I told them it was their parish. I like input and ideas. There's wisdom in the community. So we gather people once a month and all ideas are welcome. I'm always calling out the equal access of all to use their skills and gifts. No turf wars. I also give them plenty of room to exercise their creativity. It has been very collaborative. At every parish council meeting we have the time and talent cards with us as we discuss the areas of parish life."

"That's a great idea, Stephen. I've tried to keep people informed about what was going on, to be very open and not to be a dictator. As a lay leader I feel it's vitally important to have the people of the parish as involved as possible. I feel I'm putting some leadership back into the parish that had been taken away. They've been encouraged to take ownership of the church—something they didn't have an opportunity to do when the priest-pastor was there."

"That's good. I've also delegated most ministries. I see myself as a steward of the parishes, not the only one who knows anything. I'm just there to help them. I'm not the king of the parish who demands. I try not to let myself get in the way of the people who are doing all the things they should be doing."

"And sharing leadership really works. I'm finding that people are proud of the way we work together. I use a consensus model for decision making. I can't remember the last time we took a vote. Gradually, we work things out. We take time with things until consensus builds. I also believe in leadership formation and spiritual formation—especially of my catechists, staff, and council. I try to form them as a faith community and empower them."

"It's a stretching experience, isn't it, Denise? My parishioners were used to going to the priest to check if things were okay. I challenge them to be more, to do more."

"I find they're up to the challenge. I believe it's a movement of the Holy Spirit to return the church to being a church of the people."

"I'll say amen to that! Check, please."

✨

*I*t's true. Every lay Catholic who is appointed to lead a parish meets resistance and struggles, some daunting enough to discourage even faith-filled, confident people like "Denise" and "Stephen." And yet every lay parish leader who was interviewed agreed that the Spirit is working in this ministry. Under their leadership the baptized are taking ownership for the direction and viability of their parishes, which then grow in numbers, vitality, and solidarity. What is their secret recipe? First, they identify as equals with the people in the pew, resisting the tendency of Catholics to set apart and elevate their leaders. Second, they are committed to collaborating with and facilitating collaboration among their parishioners.

Those interviewed consistently communicate that a strategy of collaborative leadership is empowering the baptized to exercise their common priesthood. By breaking old habits of dependence and dominance and forming new habits of equality and collaboration, lay parish leaders are facilitating the full flowering of the Vatican II vision of the church as the People of God.

Life Without Father

Life in a parish without a pastor can be pretty exciting. To begin with, all kinds of issues arise that don't exist in other parishes. Some stem from a sense of vulnerability that many priestless parishes share, but most are the result of the new dynamic of having a lay leader. In all their diverse parishes, the lay leaders who were interviewed spoke of similar challenges—resistance to their leadership, personal issues, diocesan politics, and financial struggles.

Diverse parishes. A wide range of parishes is represented by the leaders interviewed for this book. One parish has twenty-two hundred families; another has about twelve. One is in the core of the city; another is secluded in the country. While some parishes consider their existence to be endangered, others have no such concerns. This has changed the analysis of lay parish leadership somewhat. It had been thought that the need to fight for survival contributed significantly to the high levels of participation in lay-led parishes (Wallace, 1992: 99). Now it seems that involvement increases under lay leaders even in parishes that are not vulnerable to being closed.

Resistance. Parishes that fear closing do, however, exhibit stronger initial acceptance of lay leaders, as do parishes that have done without a pastoral leader and those that have had a previous positive experience with a lay parish leader. The interviewee who received the least resistance of all is the person who had worked in the parish for several years before her appointment. Lay leaders who succeeded resident priest-pastors expressed receiving the most resistance to their leadership. Some interviewees said that their lack of ordination was problematic for only a few parishioners who soon found other parishes to join.

In some situations, pressures on the parish made acceptance of a lay leader more difficult. Some lay leaders cited a parish merger, financial instability, internal divisions, and the norms of the surrounding culture. Cultural expectations of young women exacerbated the resistance to one young female lay leader who was interviewed. After an initial period of resistance, however, all the lay leaders interviewed have enjoyed deep appreciation and acceptance from the parishioners they serve.

Personal issues. Among the internal challenges that lay leaders face, interviewees most often mentioned difficulty setting boundaries, saying no, and taking time off. They acutely feel the pressure to be available "24/7." They also struggle to stay current with the various areas of ministry for which they are held accountable. There is a sense that balancing their desire to "pastor" with their own personal needs is a constant, worthwhile issue for lay parish leaders and their parishes. One person said that attending to his own and his family's needs helps motivate him to delegate activities that rightfully should be entrusted to parishioners.

Diocesan politics. On the one hand, the most significant external pressures on lay leaders come from diocesan systems and from their relationships with clergy. Those interviewed have struggled with exclusion from diocesan decision making, lack of support from diocesan personnel, lack of information, and negative attitudes from deacons, priests, and bishops. On the other hand, clergy, diocesan personnel, diocesan meetings, and other lay leaders provide both spiritual and practical support to many of the lay leaders who were interviewed. These factors have a profound impact on their ability to minister fruitfully in their parishes. They will be discussed more fully in the next two chapters.

Financial struggles. Salary, benefits, and length of contract are areas in which tension erupts between lay leaders and their parishes. In the small sample of people interviewed, only one feels her salary is appropriate to her level of responsibility and adequate to meet her family's needs. A few are working for part-time salaries and need to work elsewhere to supplement their income. All expressed uncertainty about whether they would have a job next year, something especially unnerving for someone supporting a family. These struggles are shared by many lay ministers in the church, but the situation of lay parish leaders points to the inequity of a system that seems to find more than adequate resources to support its clergy.

Empowerment. In spite of their struggles, all the lay leaders interviewed say their parishes appreciate their leadership and, in fact, are now healthier than ever. This finding was confirmed by both the Institute for Pastoral Life (Burkart, 86) and by Ruth Wallace, a sociologist who studied parishes led by laywomen over a decade ago. Her book, *They Call Her Pastor*, found an "increase in numbers, contributions and participation in parish life . . . and a growing spirit of solidarity within the parish" (Wallace, 92: 120, 81).

What is the cause of this increased participation? Many interviewees spoke of the positive effects of their presence, accessibility, positive attitude, spiritual nourishment, and organization in the parish. But they point to their lay perspective as the single most significant factor in their ability to enliven the congregation. Although one might expect that their lack of ordination would present an obstacle to their leadership, parish life blossoms in response to their identification with parishioners as equals.

"Equal Access"

Lay perspective. The lay leaders interviewed attribute their success largely to their lay perspective. It affects everything they do, from preaching to the way they relate to parishioners. Some emphasize their married status as a real asset in ministry. This factor is currently being explored by Ruth Wallace in a controlled study of Catholic parishes led by married deacons and married laymen. Her results may be available in early 2003. Other interviewees find that their experience as parents, or simply their need to support themselves, links them to parishioners and improves their preaching.

Equality. There is a deeper issue here than simply being able to draw on shared experience to facilitate ministry. Parishioners have said that they feel more comfortable expressing their opinions and exercising their gifts with a lay leader than with a priest. They feel their lay leaders are "one of them." Leaders and parishioners stand side by side as equals. In fact, the lay leaders interviewed deliberately emphasize their equality with parishioners. They structure parish life to foster "equal access" and equal responsibility for the parish's life and ministry. They feel this commitment to equal access is key to empowering all the baptized to collaborate in the work of the church.

New dynamic. Wallace's study corroborates the evidence from these few lay leaders. She emphasizes their "new leadership style that incorporates their parishioners as peers. . . . Decisions tend to be made in a democratic and participatory mode, where all are perceived as equal." She found that when presiding at liturgical services, many of the women "argued against ever accepting . . . even an alb because they identify very strongly with the laity." Wallace theorizes that both the "clerical socialization process" of priests and the tendency of Catholic laity to put priests on a pedestal inhibit the full empowerment of the baptized. "It may be that a lay pastor will be more effective in restructuring the parish than a priest, because a priest's presence may intimidate parishioners and inhibit their adoption of a new way of thinking about the church" (Wallace, 1992: 171, 100, 130, 71, 88).

Others have pointed out this curious dynamic between Catholic clergy and laity. Noted liturgist Father Joseph Gelineau said that in France "lay people will only take pastoral responsibility in the actual absence of a priest" (Michel, 1989: 31). "A sobering realization of the extent of the Gospel's challenge and the courage it takes to live the Christian life is awakened in laity who find that they are the church, and that there are no priests . . . to whom to give over that burdensome gift" (Killen, 1988: 109). When there is no resident priest-pastor, there is no one to place on a pedestal, no one to expect to do the thinking and the work for the people. Parishioners are challenged to take responsibility for the mission of the church. No one can claim to be set apart and no one can claim to be unworthy or unqualified when the baptized lead the baptized.

A Framework for Interpretation

Ronald Heifetz directs the Leadership Education Project at Harvard University. In his book *Leadership without Easy Answers,* Heifetz provides a framework for understanding why the decidedly lay perspective of these parish leaders is so significant. It has to do with the way all groups relate to their authority figures. He says that human societies expect their authorities to "protect, direct and order" their life together (Heifetz, 1994: 69). Authority figures commonly act as "experts" trying to fix all the problems that surface in the group.

The Tried. Most Catholics have had firsthand experience with this relational pattern in the church. Here the group (i.e., the parish) relinquishes all accountability for their safety, direction, and operation to the lofty leader (i.e., the pastor). The heroic hierarch (i.e., Father) dutifully dons the royal mantle (i.e., clerical garb) and wields the scepter (i.e., shepherd's staff) of responsibility for rescuing the members (i.e., the laity) from every problem that arises—keeping them safe from harm, telling them where they must go, and showing them how to get there. Since "Father knows best," all the group needs to do is to follow. In return, the revered leader is lifted up in awe and showered with gratitude.

The True. This is not at all what Heifetz defines as true leadership. He says true leaders "mobilize" people to do "adaptive work" (Heifetz, 1994: 22f.). In other words, a true leader is not a hero who protects the group from all evils or an expert who fixes all their problems. A true leader helps the group to recognize and respond to whatever challenges arise. Leaders begin this process by failing the expectations of the group—refusing to play the hero/expert role. Heifetz says a leader must then provide just enough security, vision, and structure so that the group will have the courage to work together to adapt to challenging situations that emerge.

Leadership among equals. These two models of leadership illuminate what happens when a layperson leads a Catholic parish. Lay leaders are being appointed as a temporary "fix" to protect the church from the problem of the priest shortage. If they were to accept this official view of the situation, they might simply replicate the functioning of the priest-pastors whose shoes they are supposed to fill. But lay parish leaders are not inclined to rush in as hero/experts to plug the gap created by the lack of priest-pastors. They are refusing to perpetuate that well-worn relational pattern. They back away from the pedestal left vacant by Father's absence. They shirk the collar that can leash those it elevates to sole responsibility for the "salvation" and mission of the church. Instead, they are humbly keeping their feet on the "humus" and their eyes level with all of the baptized.

Lay leaders do not see the lack of a pastor as a problem for them to fix single-handedly, but as a challenge for the community to face together. Thus, they feel a mandate to empower parishioners to adapt to their changed situation by claiming the priesthood and pastorhood of Christ that all the baptized share. To this end lay leaders are exercising what Heifetz describes as true leadership. Instead of protecting the group from their problems, they are revealing the challenges to which the group must adapt. Instead of directing, they are enabling the group to decide how they will respond. Instead of ordering, they are facilitating the group's shared work of adapting to their changed situation.

This "lay" attitude and style of leadership exemplifies the current understanding of collaborative leadership so highly valued in church circles today. Heifetz helps us to see why collaboration in the church must begin with a deeply rooted sense of equality between leaders and the community. In the words of Cardinal Roger Mahoney, "True collaboration requires . . . a clear recognition of the fundamental equality of all the baptized, ordained and nonordained" (Mahoney, *Origins*, May 4, 2000: 750).

Collaborative Leadership

As our brief glimpse of Heifetz's leadership theory suggests, a sense of equality alone is not enough to empower a community. The person in authority must also truly lead. What does effective leadership in a parish entail? Cardinal Mahoney sounds very much like Ronald Heifetz as he identifies the pastoral leader's role in collaboration: "the pastor seeks to discern, call forth, animate and send forth his parishioners to serve the needs of the people. [He is] not the one who does it all" (Mahoney, *Origins*, May 4, 2000: 746). The fictitious conversation that opened this chapter quotes most of the strategies that those interviewed say they use to empower their parishioners—strategies that match Cardinal Mahoney's description of collaborative leadership. The list is long.

Strategies. In broad strokes, the lay leaders I interviewed seek to create an atmosphere of mutual respect for each person's dignity and shift ownership of the church's mission to the parishioners. They talk about encouraging everyone to contribute to decision-making processes by sharing information and welcoming ideas. They place a high priority on educating parishioners to understand their calling as members of the baptized. They seek out processes to discern and structures to utilize the gifts of all to serve the needs of the church and the wider community. They try to publicly recognize those who serve. They share leadership and power by delegating, enabling, supporting, stewarding—and "getting out of the way." They aim at facilitating the collaboration of parishioners with one another in every aspect of parish life.

Definition. These same strategies have surfaced in Ruth Wallace's study of lay parish leaders and in almost every discussion of "collaboration," "collaborative ministry," or "collaborative leadership" in the church today. Two definitions of this leadership style will help us gain a richer sense of the nature of collaboration. Wallace paints a fluid and circular picture of collaborative leadership as relationships "based on equality rather than hierarchy," in which all work together to achieve a common end and "the leader guides rather than commands," while drawing on the talents of others (Wallace, 1992: 67). In their very practical book on collaboration, Brother Loughlan Sofield and Sister Carroll Juliano define collaborative ministry like an arrow shot from a bow: "The essence of collaborative ministry is identifying, releasing, and uniting all the gifts present in the community for the sake of mission" (Sofield, 2000: 153).

Tasks. Sofield and Juliano cite many sources of guidance on the tasks of leaders who wish to foster collaboration. Bishop Howard Hubbard of Albany, New York, reminds pastoral leaders of the need to: (1) help people recognize their baptismal call to ministry, (2) help all to discern their gifts and how to use them in service, and (3) "challenge all leaders to see their primary role as empowering and animating the gifts of the entire community" (Sofield, 2000: 22). Bishop Hubbard's first point highlights the power of educating all the baptized to a renewed understanding of their role in the church. His third challenge recognizes that all who lead—priests, professionals, and volunteer leaders—must be committed to collaboration in parish life.

One example of a key volunteer leadership ministry is the parish pastoral council. The Canadian Conference of Catholic Bishops identifies three major tasks of pastoral councils: "(1) to identify needs; (2) to discern the gifts and resources available; and (3) to establish the structures to bring about a marriage between the needs and gifts/resources" (Sofield, 2000: 22, 160). There are two significant lessons here. The first is the importance of beginning where all ministry should—with the needs to be met. The second is the need to create structures that will enable the baptized to use their gifts in service—no matter who might be in leadership next year!

Evaluation. Sofield and Juliano list several factors that most influence the success of collaboration:

1. a history of collaboration;
2. mutual respect, understanding, and trust;
3. representation of all groups in the parish;
4. recognition that collaboration is in everyone's self-interest;
5. all members sharing a stake in the outcome;
6. shared layers of decision making;
7. open and frequent communication;

8. establishment of links between people and activities;
9. attainable goals;
10. adequate funds;
11. and skilled leaders (Sofield, 2000: 173–174).

Since lack of any of the above factors inhibits the ability of a community to collaborate for mission, leaders who seek to foster collaboration can use them as a checklist for evaluating attitudes, structures, and processes in parish life. The lay leaders quoted by Denise and Stephen at the beginning of this chapter voiced a concern for many of these factors. They seek to act as "skilled leaders" and to enable others to share the task of leading all the baptized in collaborative ministry.

Responding to the one Spirit that binds them as equal collaborators with the whole People of God, baptized yet nonordained leaders are fostering responsiveness to that same Spirit of equal dignity and responsibility in the church. Through their emphasis on equality and collaboration they are facilitating the common priesthood of believers in those they lead. The People of God are owning their responsibility to respect one another as equals, to witness the solidarity to which all God's people are called and to join together as coworkers in service to the world.

The Equality of All the Baptized

People of God. By canon law all the baptized share "a true equality regarding dignity and action by which they all cooperate" (Canon 208, Beal, 2000: 258). Thus, *all* the baptized are equal within the one People of God and their equality enables their collaboration. But do Catholics really think that all people *should* be equal in the church? The People of God sounds like an undifferentiated mass of humanity, wandering about with each person equally able to decide what to do and equally able to shirk responsibility for the group's actions. This sounds suspiciously like anarchy.

If no one was in charge in the church, how would anything get done? If everyone was in charge, who would mop the floors? People need structure and a fearless leader to tell them the plan, don't they? There must be queen bees and worker bees, line and staff, laws, flow charts, division of labor, time clocks, and paychecks reflecting each person's real value to and responsibility for the organization—in short, hierarchy. Mustn't there? Even the Israelite People of God had Moses. And look at what happened to them—they wandered in the desert for forty years!

There are, of course, no guarantees that the church will ever stop "wandering in the desert" in this world. But the questions above highlight the limits of the image of the People of God. By itself it can't adequately support the vision of collaboration for mission that embraces the need for both equality and leadership. Yet the old pyramid-shaped model of the church obscures the equality of all the baptized. Neither anarchy nor hierarchy will suffice. Two other images will rescue us from our dilemma—the image of the church as communion that will be explored in the next two chapters, and the image of the Body of Christ.

The Body of Christ. In the People of God all the baptized are equal, uniquely gifted, and energized by the one Spirit of the one Christ to collaborate as an organic whole on behalf of the world. This is why the church is said to be the Body of Christ. Both equality and leadership find a foundation in this Pauline image of the church as a living, breathing, functioning human body. The one Body enlivened by the one Spirit models the collaboration among equals that is required among all the baptized.

It's helpful to imagine one's own body, the breath that keeps it alive, the simultaneous and coordinated working of all the organs and all the cells within these organs. When one organ malfunctions, the body can die. When one "member" is cut off, the member decays and the whole body is crippled. When one member does not get enough exercise, it withers. An illness in one system hurts the whole body.

While one might think that the head or the heart is the most important part of the body, neither alone can sustain life. And without the muscles and nerves and bones, the body cannot function as a coordinated whole to accomplish even one single task. Even the excretory system is equally vital and valuable to the body. If it were to stop functioning, the body would be poisoned and lose its life, its animating Spirit, its soul. All the members are uniquely and equally important. In order to function, the body needs all its parts interconnected and working together.

This is exactly what Paul has in mind in the twelfth chapter of his letter to the Corinthians when he says, "In the one Spirit we were all baptized into the one Body," which "does not consist of one member but of many." "There are varieties of gifts but the same Spirit" (*anima*) "animating" each gift, binding them together, and breathing life into the one living, working body to which all the members must stay connected in order to stay alive. Each member has a unique role that is "indispensable" to the body; "the eye cannot say to the hand, 'I have no need of you.'" And all the members must collaborate in the body since "if the whole body were an eye, where would the hearing be?" Every member deserves equal "honor . . . respect . . . and care," for "if one member suffers, all suffer together with it; if one member is honored, all rejoice together with it" (1 Corinthians 12:4–26).

As the Body of Christ, all the baptized are equal in dignity and importance, but all are not the same. "Not all are eyes; not all are feet." They function in various ways in concert with one another. All are equal, but all are not self-sufficient. No Christian can survive if cut off from the body; and the Body of Christ is crippled when even one member of the baptized does not exercise its function. All the baptized are interdependent in a single organism that needs the collaboration of all the members to stay healthy and accomplish its mission. The head alone, the heart alone, the hand alone cannot perform the whole ministry of Christ. All are equal in importance as they unite to do the one work of the one Body of Christ.

Yet equality alone does not define the baptized. As members of the Body of Christ, the baptized are called to unite their unique gifts and collaborate in service to the body and to the world. In order for this to happen, some in the body must perform the indispensable task of leadership. This task does not and should not rest entirely on the ordained. Clergy, lay ministers, and parish members themselves must collaborate in the work of leadership to facilitate the equality, unity, and collaboration of all the members in the one Body of Christ.

Questions to Consider

- What difficulties might a lay leader encounter in your parish?
- What attitudes would help a lay minister effectively lead your parish?
- How important are questions of wages and contracts for lay ministers? Explain.
- What differences do you notice in the way lay and ordained ministers relate to parishioners?
- Would you say that ordained and lay ministers treat you as their equal? Explain.
- Who would you describe as collaborative leaders? How do they lead collaboratively?
- What strategic or structural change might increase collaboration in your parish?
- How do you "lead" or "collaborate" in your parish community?
- What attracts you to the images of the People of God and the Body of Christ?

⌒: CHAPTER 6 :⌒

What About Father?
Collaborative Ministry

*N*apping or praying, Monsignor Peters?"

"Larry Wolski! Good to see you."

"You look great, Ben."

"What brings you to the chancery offices, Father?"

"Oh, I'm here to visit some of my ex-parishioners who moved to town, so I decided to come early and bother you."

"Glad you did. What's new out in the boondocks?"

"Not much. I was hoping we could talk about my assignment as a—'sacramental minister?' I don't like it."

"Well, Larry, if you and Stephen are having problems, we can move you. We've done it before. But I haven't heard any complaints. Things must be going pretty well."

"They are, I guess, but I don't think I know how to do this—or want to know how."

"What do you mean?"

"I really don't understand my role now. My background didn't prepare me for this 'sacramental stud' status. Who am I if I'm not the pastor, the agenda setter?"

"I know what you mean. It was hard for me to adjust. You have to re-envision what it means to be a priest. But I know one thing— we're not supposed to be just sacrament machines. We need rootedness in a parish family, too. I've worked hard to cultivate relationships in the parish where I celebrate the sacraments, and I actually feel as though it's my faith community now. Although it's hard to do this without falling into the pastor role again."

"That's just it. If the pastoral administrators make the parish decisions and do all the pastoral care, what's left for us? Stephen is so smart and capable and caring; I think the folks respect him more than they respect me. He's the one who's there for them. I have trouble just remembering their names. But I don't begrudge him. I know it's not really about Stephen; it's about me. I'd have trouble with anyone. And blaming doesn't help. To be honest, Ben, I find myself feeling pretty vulnerable and defensive about my priesthood more often than I want to admit. Especially in areas of ministry where I haven't kept up over the years."

"We're all susceptible to that. Maybe it's easier for me because I have some authority here in the chancery, but it's tough. At the parish I feel like I'm on the sidelines, the cheerleader instead of the quarterback."

"You hit the nail on the head, Ben. Actually, I think I'm a darned good cheerleader. I always tell Stephen he's doing great. I try not to step on his toes, you know? And I've started praying for him in the Eucharistic Prayer on Sundays."

"That's a great idea. Can I share it with the other guys?"

"Sure. I guess I'm doing what I'm supposed to do. Only it doesn't square with my expectations. I entered the priesthood with an image of myself as pastor. I believed that when I became pastor I would lead my people to the fullness of what God wants for them. Now I'm not a pastor, but just a 'sacramental minister.' How can I be a priestly person without being a pastor? We're supposed to be 'priests, prophets, and kings.' I can't imagine how I can exercise the prophetic and kingly aspects of my vocation without pastoring."

"It's difficult for me, too. It's as though there's an emotional or psychological need in me that goes unmet. Larry, we'll all still get to be pastors during our priestly life. But we'll have to spend some time as sacramental ministers, too, at least for the foreseeable future. I look at it this way—it's all there in the liturgy. Sacraments are the most regal and prophetic moments in the church's faith life. The ordained priest within the liturgy embodies the fullness of priestly, prophetic, and royal ministry for the church."

"You're right, of course. I tell myself at least I'm not tied down to administrative responsibilities like I would be if I had to pastor all three of these parishes. I sure don't think I was ordained to worry about broken steam pipes. It does leave me more time and energy for prayer, sacraments, to be with people at the important times. We do more than enough paper shuffling in the presbyteral council, if you ask me."

"I hear you, Larry. You know, all this can feel like it's undermining our authority and credibility as priests, but I think it may be helping us define more clearly the identity of priesthood. The bishop says that encouraging laypeople to use the gifts they have for the service of the community will help people better understand the ordained as well as the priesthood of the faithful. The 'complementarity of gifts.' I believe that."

"Well, I can tell you for certain, Ben, that not all our brother priests agree with you and the bishop. I don't know what to make of this reemerging clericalism, especially in some of the younger guys. I'm ashamed of the way a few of them treat the pastoral administrators. It's as though these people have to prove their orthodoxy to them!"

"Maybe they'll come around. Remember in the early days when all the pastoral administrators were nuns and we used to say they were just angry women? We learned that they're not angry, they're dedicated, and they're doing a great job. The more they share with us at deanery meetings, continuing ed. days, the more similarity and partnership we discover. Really, they're in a very good position to break down walls between clergy and laity through their intimate interaction with us. It's challenging, though—their different lifestyles, points of view, the questions they ask of us. I think it's good for everybody."

"Also hard for everybody. And threatening. The image of Father isn't coming back. It feels like a relational thing. With laypeople leading parishes we have to redefine our relationships with everybody in the church."

"What we need are collaborative relationships, if you ask me. The pastoral administrator and the sacramental minister should work as a team. It takes a real spirit of collaboration to avoid turfdom, because you and I know that that's not only a clerical thing. We need a spirit of service to the people and the Lord."

"Well, Stephen and I sure try to model team leadership to the parish. It forces me to get out of the rut of solo leadership, to see how we all need to work together. Maybe this is a good start."

"Sure it is. It's shared accountability. We're reimagining church in a shared ministry model where 'one does not Lord it over another.' It's living the Gospel and Paul's letters with the whole thing of recognizing the Body of Christ in the church."

"Back to our roots? Okay, I admit this might be good for us. Good for me. But why does everything good for me have to hurt or taste like cardboard? Thanks for the ear, Ben."

"Anytime, Larry. Enjoy your day in the city."

⚬

*H*ow are priests responding to the ministry of lay parish leaders? Clearly, this ministry has a tremendous impact on them, as this fictitious conversation between two clerical characters illustrates. Some of the words quoted here come from priests who are serving as sacramental ministers; others come from lay parish leaders, parishioners, and diocesan coordinators. Many priests find that being a sacramental minister shakes their previously firm self-identity. Some genuinely fear the effects that lay parish leadership might have on the church. Other priests rejoice to welcome laypeople as pastoral collaborators. They perceive the Spirit at work in lay leadership and appreciate being able to share their ever-expanding list of pastoral tasks.

Through this phenomenon the whole church is being challenged to refine the distinction between what is called "priestly identity" and the identity of the baptized. Priests are summoned to claim a more nuanced understanding of their pastoral ministry. The ministry of lay parish leaders leads them to embrace collaborative ministry as the pastor's fundamental task, one that can lead all the baptized to reflect more truly the image of the church as a communion of creative love. Lay Catholics in turn are led to relate to "Father" no longer as children but as full-grown, capable, responsible adults.

Laypeople are being appointed to lead the lay Catholics in their parishes. Yet they are also leading the ordained Catholics with whom they collaborate. Lay parish leaders, in fact, are leading all the baptized.

"Sacrament Machines"

In the opening conversation, "Larry" and "Ben" laid bare the range of experiences and responses of priests who minister with lay parish leaders. Many of their words come from the diocesan coordinators and priests who were interviewed. They were especially helpful in explaining the priests' perspective on this ministry. The lay leaders who were interviewed spoke from their perspective about their interactions with those whom one lay leader called their "brother priests."

Priests' perspective. In most dioceses, priests who celebrate sacraments with parishes that are led by laypersons are called sacramental ministers. The title reflects many of the difficulties inherent in this role. Priests can feel like sacrament machines, valued only for the "candy" they dispense in one congregation after another. Many spend long hours traveling from parish to parish. It is common for sacramental ministers to have two or more assignments. Some, like "Monsignor Peters," also work in diocesan (or chancery) offices. Others might provide sacraments at several parishes or be assigned as pastor to one parish and sacramental minister to one or two others.

Ruth Wallace is not the only researcher who has noted that sacramental ministers commonly feel disconnected from parish life, saying that the Christian community can easily become "just faces" to them (Wallace, 1992: 53, 57). Many, like our "Father Wolski," feel marginalized and grieve the loss of a ministry that has been a vital part of their priestly lives. One priest who was interviewed said that the burden is on the priests to cultivate relationships with the communities they serve. Yet a diocesan coordinator said that some priests find it hard to relate in any other way than as pastor or agenda setter.

One interviewee noted that the "inadequacy" of their background keeps some priests from understanding the change in their role. Wallace conjectures that "their training leaves them ill equipped," particularly for "dealing with women as colleagues" (Wallace, 1992: 159). The U.S. Bishops' Subcommittee on Lay Ministry found similar concerns among the bishops they interviewed. Bishops asked how they could "prepare and educate priests for greater involvement of the laity" and how to "convince our people (perhaps priests) that lay ministry is not second-class ministry?" (Committee on the Laity, 1999: 45, 46, parenthetical insert included in the original).

It may be a difficult task since many men come to the seminary carrying with them "a rigid understanding of their faith." In her careful study, *Seminaries, Theologates and the Future of Church Ministry*, Sister Katarina Schuth describes how these same men create a climate of distrust and defensiveness . . . questioning the orthodoxy of professors and fellow students (Schuth, 1999: 77). This attitude is not, unfortunately, confined to seminarians.

The diocesan coordinators interviewed admitted that a significant number of clergy see lay parish leaders as very problematic and undermining both the authority and credibility of the priesthood. As a result, some priests feel threatened by the ministry of lay parish leaders and tend to judge and exclude them. These priests feel it is their duty to test the orthodoxy of and limit the "damage" (i.e., ministry) done by lay parish leaders. Perhaps this is because, as one diocesan coordinator indicated, this ministry challenges the clergy's self-understanding.

One priest who was interviewed, however, feels that lay parish leaders are helping priests claim their true identity and role. Rather than being overloaded with administrative tasks, they can spend their time in sacramental ministry. And, as their experience with lay leaders grows, more and more priests are seeing lay leaders as partners in ministry. One priest emphasized the importance of genuine collaboration between clergy and laity, noting that both sides can tend to protect their own "turf." Yet almost unanimously, those interviewed assert that the challenge of lay/clergy collaboration is crucial to the success of lay leaders in Catholic parishes.

Lay leaders' perspective. There seems to be a real difference between the way lay leaders experience the clergy as a group and as individuals. All the lay leaders interviewed mentioned experiencing resistance from the priests and/or bishop at some diocesan meetings. They say they consistently feel they must prove themselves to the clergy and are excluded from presbyteral networks of communication simply as a matter of course. Yet only a few have had struggles with sacramental ministers over parish decisions. They commonly find sacramental ministers to be supportive and easy to work with. And, in fact, relationships with individual priests and bishops have been the chief means of support for many of the lay leaders interviewed.

One diocesan coordinator said that lay leaders are in a good position to break down walls between clergy and laypeople through their intimate interaction with priests. The lay leaders interviewed also feel they are helping the clergy learn how to collaborate in leadership and better facilitate the priesthood of the baptized. Several talked about joint efforts at collaboration with sacramental ministers. They feel such collaboration is fruitful for themselves, the priests, and especially for their parish communities. In general, all those who were interviewed believe this ministry is fostering a spirit of genuine collaboration between Catholics who are and Catholics who are not ordained.

Priestly Identity

The 1997 *Instruction on Certain Questions Regarding the Collaboration of the Non-Ordained in the Sacred Ministry of Priests* sought "to ensure the effective collaboration of the nonordained faithful in such circumstances while *safeguarding the integrity of the pastoral ministry of priests* (*Instruction*, Conclusion, italics added). What is "the pastoral ministry of priests" that the *Instruction* wishes to safeguard and that so many of the clergy feel is being threatened by the ministry of lay parish leaders?

It begins with what theologians call "priestly identity." Some fear that lay ministries in general, and lay parish leadership in particular, might result in a "progressive erosion" of the "specific nature" of the ordained priesthood (*Instruction*, Pastoral Provisions, #1.2). If distinct priestly identity rests on what priests do, then it probably is in jeopardy, given the current explosion of involvement of laypeople in ministry. However, priestly identity is not, after all, about distinct activities or appointments. Nor is it about distinct status, knowledge, holiness, or garb. It is about sacramental character, a distinct relationship to the ministry of the whole church that laypersons do not share, regardless of the functions they might perform.

Sacramental character. Ecclesiologist Susan K. Wood has written an enlightening book called *Sacramental Orders*. In her section on "presbyters," as priests are rightly called, she describes the sacramental character of priestly ordination as a representation of the whole Body of Christ by configuration to Christ, the "Head" of the Body. The ordained participate sacramentally in the relationship of Christ to the church as head of the body. Just as the whole church is represented by its head, Jesus Christ, the whole church is represented sacramentally by ordained priests. Through ordination a priest *effectively represents* ("sacramentalizes") the presence of Jesus Christ working in and through the church (Wood, 2000: 90).

Much as a head of state represents her whole country and its actions by election to a term of office, one who is "elected" by God and the church for sacramental ordination represents the whole Body of Christ. Both of these "heads of state" represent the whole people most effectively in their official capacities of governing and presiding at "state functions." For a priest, this happens by presiding at the sacraments and shepherding the mission of the church.

There are two large differences between government officeholders and church officeholders. Government officials only govern temporarily and only represent their own district (as do lay parish leaders). While the ordained *can be* appointed to govern particular parishes or dioceses temporarily, their effective representation of the church transcends such appointments: it is permanent and universal. By priestly ordination a priest becomes a "sacrament of the ecclesial community"—forever representing the whole Body of Christ throughout the world and throughout the centuries (Wood, 2000: 126). On the one hand, even if a priest is never appointed pastor, he will always sacramentally represent the ministry of the whole Body of Christ. On the other hand, no matter how many pastoral appointments laypersons receive, they will never have this relationship to the universal church.

This brief treatment doesn't begin to answer all the theological questions about priestly identity; but it does highlight the priest's permanent sacramental relationship to the whole Body of Christ, a relationship that is most effectively exercised in presiding at the church's Eucharist. A priest who acts as sacramental minister instead of pastor effectively lives out his distinct priestly identity in his life and prayers and in presiding at the sacraments, since in the sacraments, especially the Eucharist, he *effectively represents* the whole Body of Christ—head and members.

A Broader View of "Pastoring"

"The pastoral ministry of priests" may begin with sacramental priestly identity but it manifests itself in the ministry of "pastoring." Christ the Head is also Christ the Good Shepherd. Priests effectively represent Christ's shepherding of the ministry of the church. Must a priest be a parish pastor in order to manifest his priestly identity and exercise pastoral ministry? The short answer is "No." Many ordained priests are not appointed pastors; they serve in other ministries such as teaching or directing retreats. But a longer answer is in order. As previously indicated, the ordained have the responsibility of guiding and caring for (i.e., pastoring) the Catholic Church. The significant question for us to explore is: "*How* can priests exercise this pastoral responsibility without being a parish pastor?" The answer is threefold—spiritually, collegially, and collaboratively.

Spiritual leadership. Dr. Wood's work is again helpful here. She points out that the norm and ideal is for the priest who presides at a community's Eucharist to also preside over the ministry of the community as pastor. The first represents and is made more effective by the second (Wood, 2001: 147). However, this is not always the case for Catholics. Catholics are often led in worship by priests other than their pastors. It works for them because the presider at Mass represents more than just the gathered assembly. His presiding at the church's Eucharist manifests his "presiding over" the *universal* church of which the parish community is a part.

It also works because Catholics seek *spiritual* guidance and leadership from the ordained, something they receive through the homily, the Eucharist, and other sacraments. Wood admits that the *Rite of Ordination* and *Lumen gentium* both emphasize that "a presbyter's leadership is preeminently a spiritual one" that happens "above all in worship"; and again: "Among the duties of presbyter the sanctifying role predominates" (Wood, 2000: 96, 120, 103). Through sacramental ministry a priest exercises spiritual pastoral ministry in the community. Thus, *spiritual leadership* is more important to Catholics and more essential to priestly ministry than their governance of the practical affairs of a parish.

Collegial governance. Dr. Wood is careful to point out that the pastoral ministry of priests is a sharing in the pastoral office of their bishop. The whole *college* of priests in the diocese shares responsibility with the bishop for shepherding the *whole diocesan church.* A parish pastor is given special responsibility for that particular portion of the diocese, but "the government of the particular church is fundamentally *collegial . . .* and is a shared responsibility" (Wood, 2000: 127). This is what makes diocesan presbyteral councils so significant as a structure of governance in the diocese. Through their participation in the presbyteral council, *all* the priests of the diocese—even those who are not appointed as pastors—share in the *collegial governance* of the entire diocesan church.

Collaborative care. In addition to spiritual leadership and diocesan governance, pastoral ministry includes the task of providing pastoral care to the People of God. It has been noted that pastoral care is a ministry of the whole church. Lay ministers and priests often collaborate in this area of parish life. At the same time their goal should be to empower all the baptized to collaborate together in praying and caring for one another through the anxieties and sorrows of daily life.

Priests have a significant responsibility to provide pastoral care to those who give pastoral care to others. Lay parish leaders are among those who need "pastors," often the sacramental ministers with whom they work, to support and guide them in their exercise of pastoral care. While pastoral care is ultimately the responsibility of the ordained, it is not for them to provide single-handedly, but to shepherd and support others in the *collaborative* exercise of the *pastoral care* of Christ, the Good Shepherd.

The pastoral ministry of priests can be exercised in a variety of ways in a variety of situations. It normally finds expression in the role of parish pastor, but this does not have to be the case. Both the tradition and the Catholic community understand priestly ministry primarily as spiritual leadership of guidance and prayer that is exercised most fully in the sacraments. Priests' pastoral ministry also includes participation in the bishop's pastoral leadership of the diocese through collegial structures of governance. Finally, it involves pastoral care, a ministry that can and should be shared with all the baptized. Priests who function as sacramental ministers exercise their pastoral responsibility for the church in all three ways.

"Genuine Collaboration"

Vision. The ministry of priests is more and more being understood in the context of collaborative ministry. Collaborative ministry illuminates the relationship of priests to the ministry of the church. It enables the ordained to empower the priesthood of all the baptized and to lead the church to manifest more fully its nature as a communion of creative love. Even the 1997 Vatican *Instruction* on collaboration notes that:

The ministerial priesthood is *at the service of the common priesthood* and directed at the unfolding of the baptismal grace of all Christians. . . . The priest is exhorted . . . to grow in awareness of the *deep communion* uniting him to the People of God in order to awaken and deepen *co-responsibility* in the one common mission of salvation with a prompt and heartfelt *esteem for all the charisms and tasks* which the Spirit gives believers for the building up of the Church" (*Instruction*, 1997, Theological Principles, #1, italics added).

Cardinal Roger Mahoney's pastoral letter on ministry also accentuates over and over the "pressing need for greater collaboration and inclusivity in ministry in the church of the new millennium" (Mahoney, 2000: 747).

Some still fear that collaboration of priests with the merely baptized will obscure the distinct identities of clergy and laity, but the United States bishops disagree. In their 1999 statement *Lay Ecclesial Ministry*, they write, "Genuine collaboration of ordained ministers and lay ecclesial ministers diminishes neither the sacramental character of ordination nor the properly secular character of the laity, but rather enriches both" (*LEM*, 18).

Fostering collaboration. Across the nation bishops are asking how they can "foster respectful collaboration" (*CGFTM*, 18). Cardinal Mahoney echoes this call, asking, "How might we better educate seminarians and priests to recognize and develop the gifts of all the baptized?" He believes this formation must be both theological and practical: "There is a need for a common foundational theology for the formation of seminarians, deacons, religious and laypersons for ministry as well as for the development of more collaborative skills on the part of the ordained" (Mahoney, 2000: 752, 747).

One avenue for fostering collaboration is the ongoing formation of priests. Last year the United States bishops approved *The Basic Plan of Ongoing Formation for Priests*. Three aspects of the plan can help priests engage in collaborative ministry. Rev. Louis J. Cameli, principal writer for the plan, points out first that "the basic plan highlights the communal aspects of priestly ministry and life." Cameli also recognizes that priests today are living in "a moment of adventure in faith, a movement forward into uncharted territory. We know that God accompanies us and leads us but we are reluctant." The plan thus calls for ongoing formation to help priests welcome change and live in hope: to "willingly embrace a dynamic, growing and moving sense of priestly ministry and life" and "to live permanently and patiently with a promise that is slowly and surely being fulfilled" (Cameli, *Origins*, April 26, 2001: 724, 725, 726). Ongoing formation that fosters a communal sense of ministry, openness to change, and hope for the future will support priests in their efforts to engage in collaborative ministry.

Another avenue is seminary training. The Vatican *Instruction* on collaboration expresses the need to "ensure a proper seminary training" (Theological Principles, #3). At the same time it assures its bishop-readers that it is not "concern[ed] to defend clerical privileges" (Conclusion). What kind of seminary training will "ensure effective collaboration" and avoid defending "clerical privileges"?

Cardinal Mahoney has called a sense of equality the basis for all true collaboration. Lay parish leaders have demonstrated that when leaders identify as equals with all the baptized, they can break old patterns of work avoidance and enable the priesthood of the faithful. Since empowering the common priesthood is the expressed purpose of the ordained priesthood, it seems that proper seminary training might balance the formation of distinct priestly identity with a nurturing of the baptismal identity that ordination candidates hold in common with the whole People of God. To focus exclusively on the identity that flows from priestly ordination may run the risk of unintentionally fostering in them an undue sense of "clerical privileges."

Ordained vocations flower from and symbolize the priesthood of the whole Christian community. "Clerical privileges" should not be allowed to obscure this life-giving connection. Priestly formation that nurtures a sense of common identity with all the baptized could counteract such tendencies, foster effective collaboration, empower the common priesthood of the baptized, and, ultimately, clarify the true sacramental character of ordination.

Models of collaboration. What models of collaborative ministry can we find? Again, we need look no further than Jesus, Paul, and their companions. Neither Jesus nor Paul tried to minister alone. Both embraced their common identification with the people and gathered others to work with them for the kingdom. Like Jesus and the Twelve who collaborated in ministry, those who lead the church must collaborate among themselves to foster collaboration throughout the church. Like Jesus, they cannot be afraid to withdraw, trusting the baptized to minister in their absence. Like Paul, they must support and laud their many collaborators in Christ. Jesus and Paul show lay and ordained ministers how to lead, not as lone rangers, but in a spirit of collaborative ministry.

Genuine collaboration does not obscure the identity of the ordained, it illuminates it. Collaborative ministry does not compete with the proper vocation of the baptized, it enables it. A vision of collaboration among equals does not jeopardize "the constitutive form" of Christ's church; it reveals the nature of the church as communion—something that "clerical privileges" only serve to conceal (*Instruction*, Conclusion). Constant attention is needed by both clergy and laity in order to keep the weeds of division that are rooted in the church's ecclesiology, organizational systems, and relational patterns from choking off the fruit of genuine collaboration. The next chapter will address some of those efforts.

The Collaboration of All the Baptized

Thus far, we have focused on the relationship between priests and lay ministers in the church. Priests like Ben and Larry are showing Catholics that the most appropriate and fruitful relationship between lay and ordained ministers today is one of genuine collaboration. Their engagement in collaborative ministry is helping the church understand the character and ministry of the ordained as both distinct from and rooted in the priesthood of the baptized. Especially in parishes with lay leaders, genuine collaboration between clergy and laity is empowering the priesthood of all the baptized.

What about the relationship between ordained and ordinary Catholics? How does all this affect the common Catholic in the pew? When priests and lay ministers embrace a vision of collaborative ministry, *all* Catholics are challenged to rethink the relationship between the ordained and the merely baptized. *All* the baptized are called to enter into this dynamic of collaboration—clergy and laity, professionals and volunteers, parish leaders and once-a-week Catholics. How does this happen?

Adult relationships. When leaders change their way of leading, the whole system has to adjust. What happens to parishioners when Father fails their expectations for him to play the hero/expert? How do ordinary Catholics respond when he says "I don't know" or "What shall we do"? Chances are the laity resist with all their might! It is much easier to place all the responsibility for the church on the hierarchy—and all the blame. It is tempting to forever play the helpless children who need to hold Father's hand. And yet the call to collaboration is a call to religious adulthood. As *Lumen gentium* explains the role of a pastor, it sounds like a mother bird pushing the chicks out of the nest and chirping, "Fly!":

> The pastors, indeed, should *recognize and promote the dignity and responsibility* of the laity . . . *confidently assign duties* to them . . . leaving them *freedom and scope for acting* . . . give them courage to *undertake works on their own initiative.* . . . The sense of *their own responsibility* is strengthened in the laity, their *zeal* is encouraged, they are more ready to *unite their energies to the work of their pastors.* . . . Strengthened by *all her members,* the Church can thus *more effectively fulfill her mission* for the life of the world" (*LG,* #37, italics added).

The message is clear: The church family has grown up. As mature, capable adults, lay Catholics are being challenged to take more responsibility than when they were "children." It is a vision of church in which *all* are adults, and the baptized must discover how to collaborate as adults with their spiritual "parents." Of course, sometimes it is the parents who resist, trying to keep their adult children "in the nest." No matter. Ordained and nonordained faithful are summoned to work side by side as equals—each respecting the other's unique gifts and roles—to fulfill the mission of Christ in the world. *All* the baptized will thereby be empowered to participate fully in the pastoral ministry of Jesus Christ in and through and beyond their parish communities.

Communion. This vision reflects the image of Paul's churches in which the members of the Body of Christ took mutual responsibility for the life and work of the Christian community. It also reflects the church's identity as a "sacrament of communion" (*LG*, #1). The bishops' synod on the laity discerned that communion is the underlying vision of the church in the documents of Vatican II. John Paul II's apostolic letter *Christifideles Laici* describes this vision.

Through communion with Christ in the Holy Spirit all the baptized "commune" with the life of love in the Trinity. The church is meant to reflect the communion of the Trinity—a mutual sharing of love and work among equal, distinct persons which issues forth in creative love for the world. This is how Catholics understand the mystery of God and it helps us understand the mystery of the church. Genuine collaboration among equals leads *all* Catholics—lay and ordained—to participate more deeply in the life and work of the triune God who is a communion of creative love.

Through the collaboration of priests and lay parish leaders, the Spirit is inviting all the baptized to embrace a relationship of communion for the life of the world.

> Pope John Paul II, in an address to a group of American bishops on July 2, 1993, gave this challenge to parishes: . . . "renew parish life in the image of the church herself as a communion benefiting from the complementary gifts and charisms of

all her members. . . . The vitality of a parish depends on merging the diverse vocations and gifts of its members into a unity which manifests the communion of each one and of all together with God" (Coriden, 1997: 122).

For the vision of the church as communion to take flesh in Catholic parishes as genuine collaboration, the church needs mature leaders, both lay and ordained, whose fully formed self-identity, trust in the Spirit, and fidelity to the church enable them to focus together on empowering all the faithful to collaborate in living out their common priestly vocation. Such collaboration requires structures that can support equality, participation, and mutual respect for one another's gifts. The next chapter will explore the essential role of dioceses in shepherding this process. When lay and ordained leaders can truly collaborate as equals, the church will harvest the fully ripened fruit of the baptized leading the baptized.

Questions to Consider

- How do you think the priests you know would respond to being assigned as sacramental ministers? How would they receive, interact with, and offer support to lay leaders?
- How can a parish involve its sacramental ministers in the life of the community?
- Who "pastors" you and how?
- How have you experienced lay and ordained ministers collaborating well?
- How do you collaborate? What attitudes or practices inhibit collaboration?
- How would you like to see seminarians trained for ministry?
- What might Catholics do if ordained or lay ministers try to keep them "in the nest"?
- What do you see when you envision your parish as a communion of creative love?

CHAPTER 7

What Is the Role of the Diocese?

Catholic Communion

*A*s the bishop finished his phone call, Sister Charlotte gathered her thoughts. She had been preparing for this meeting all week.

"I apologize for keeping you waiting, Sister Charlotte."

"Don't mention it, Bishop. We have only one thing on our agenda today—pastoral administrators."

"Yes. If I'm not mistaken, we now have nine pastoral administrators, of whom two are deacons and seven are laypersons. I'd like to review our policies and hear your ideas on how we can better facilitate their work. I'm especially concerned about promoting a true working communion between our pastoral administrators and our priests in the pastoral care of the diocese. It's too easy for pastoral administrators to become isolated and focus entirely on what's happening in their own parishes. Tell me again how we're deciding which parishes receive pastoral administrators."

"We've focused on parish vulnerability as the criterion for appointing pastoral administrators, so they've been assigned almost exclusively to the smallest and poorest parishes. It seems to me that this policy has created a separate, second class of parishes served by second-class leaders—pastoral administrators, that is. This can be divisive and demeaning. I'd like to broaden the range of parishes that receive pastoral administrators. Perhaps every parish in the diocese should have an opportunity to experience a pastoral administrator over a certain period of time."

"Interesting. See if you can find some information on dioceses that have implemented similar policies and bring it to the pastoral personnel board for their consideration. How is the appointment process working? I don't want a repeat of what happened with our first pastoral administrator."

"When we announced the appointment two weeks after the pastor had retired and the parishioners were sure their parish was closing? I hope that never happens again! Things are working smoothly. We include the parish at every step along the way."

"Perhaps you could ask the last three parishes involved to give you feedback on the process."

"I'd be glad to."

"Any suggestions regarding how we facilitate the pastoral administrators' transition into the parishes?"

"I thought we could follow up with 'town meetings' in the parishes after they've had pastoral administrators for six months or so. We could get their feedback on the appointment process at the same time."

"That'd be wonderful, Sister. Although I believe the best thing we can do to facilitate the transition is to prepare the priests for serving as sacramental ministers. That's a higher priority for me. I feel they deserve some spiritual formation and skill development for their new role, and I think the parishes would benefit from any preparation we can give the priests. I'd like to propose that to the presbyteral council and get their ideas."

"Certainly."

"Does the commissioning ritual need updating?"

"I think it's great. I can show the ritual to the folks in the worship office to see if they have any suggestions."

"Yes, good. I'd also like John to think about how we can make pastoral administrators visible at the Chrism Mass. Ask him if we could pray for them as pastoral leaders at that liturgy and allow them to renew their commitment to collaborate in the pastoral care of the diocese."

"I'll ask. Are there other ways we could publicly affirm them?"

"I've finally succeeded in having the greeting on diocesan correspondence changed from 'Dear Father' to 'Dear Pastoral Leader'—long overdue. Would you check diocesan ministry lists, communications, rituals, and such to be certain the pastoral administrators are included as a ministry group? And I'd like to see an article on them in the diocesan newspaper. Perhaps we could get the *Tribune* to do a feature on them, too."

"An article in the *Tribune* would challenge the other denominations to rethink their view of Catholics—and the role of women in the church. Of course, it would also be sure to point out any inequities in pay, benefits, job security, et cetera."

"Well, if there are financial inequities, they should be exposed and addressed. Yours is a good case in point. We tried to make your remuneration package equivalent to that of Msgr. Peters. I'll ask the diocesan finance council and staff to review the pastoral administrator contracts. I realize that many of these parishes are quite poor, but I want to help them—and us—bring greater justice in employment policies. How are we supporting the pastoral administrators otherwise?"

"They're finding the diocesan policies and pastoral administrators' meetings quite helpful. Many are also supported by their deans and deanery meetings, but others say they have to fight for respect in their regions."

"It saddens me to hear that. How can we enhance their relationships with the priests?"

"Well, I agree with you that we should better prepare the priests—all of them, since they are all affected by this ministry. The deans and sacramental ministers especially might appreciate some guidance on how to support the pastoral administrators and build healthy relationships with them. And here's another thought. Currently, one of the continuing education days each year is open to pastoral administrators but the other is strictly for priests. We could invite everyone to both sessions, but sometimes have dual tracks to meet their different needs."

"That idea will meet resistance from my brother priests."

"Yes, Bishop, I know. Some pastoral administrators have told me how difficult the large meetings can be. They feel marginalized. They say they need to work hard for their voices to be heard; otherwise, their input is just forgotten. Is there anything we can do to increase their participation in diocesan decision-making processes?"

"I really don't think so. They already have membership on most of the councils in the diocese. Our diocesan pastoral council sets direction and priorities, and two pastoral administrators are members of that group. By church law they cannot be on the presbyteral council, but Msgr. Peters represents their point of view on that board. Besides, if decisions about parish life need to be made, the priests always bring them up at meetings when the pastoral administrators are present and free to comment. Granted, priests regularly 'consult' among themselves behind the scenes; but these informal conversations happen through fraternal networks of which lay leaders are just not a part."

"Bishop, let me be frank. I realize that no malice or discrimination is intended by such 'networks,' but, intended or not, it still amounts to clericalism. I'm dismayed that we as a church still seem to place most of the ministry and power in the hands of the clergy. And I am most disappointed when it doesn't seem to be a ministry of service, when we focus on how we can serve this elite group rather than how we can, together, best serve the needs of the church and minister to the world."

"But, Charlotte, you know that's not what we're trying to do. I honestly don't see any options. We've had a largely clerical model for so long that it's hard to think in other categories. What would you advise?"

"I think you're already doing a lot. Could I address this issue at the upcoming pastoral administrators' meeting and solicit their suggestions? Perhaps they'd be willing to present a report to the presbyterate on their ministry and their experiences with the priests of the diocese."

"That can only help. I wish I could develop more of a relationship with these people, as I do with the priests. Let's talk about possibilities next month."

"Gladly. Your leadership on this issue is irreplaceable. You know, when you retire, our next bishop may not be interested in pastoral administrators at all. He may consider them theologically incorrect. In that case there would be little future for them in this diocese."

"It won't be from lack of need! What a system we have, that local church practice depends so heavily on one person who happens to be named bishop. Well, that's all the more reason for us to provide institutional support for their unity with the presbyterate while I'm here. Thank you, Sister Charlotte. Thank you for everything."

"Thank you, Bishop. Pray for the church."

"I always do."

⅋

*T*he presence of lay parish leaders in a diocese can be a powerful impetus for reform since it shines a spotlight on any inequality or exclusivity in the institutional church. They challenge everyone—including the bishop—to scrutinize diocesan networks of communication, habits of thinking and behaving, and structures of consultation in a collaborative light.

As "Sister Charlotte" just reminded her fictional bishop, bishops play an irreplaceable role in promoting—or undermining—the ministry of lay parish leaders in their dioceses. While the words quoted in this conversation did not come from the mouths of bishops, they represent the variety of ways in which actual bishops and diocesan leaders are seeking to supply institutional support for lay leaders. Many of these methods have been mentioned in previous chapters.

This chapter will focus on how diocesan leadership, policies, procedures, and structures can foster not just the ministry of lay leaders, but genuine collaboration and true communion throughout the diocese.

The parish is not the only level of the institutional church that is being called by Pope John Paul II to "renew [its] life in the image of the church herself as a communion." Bishops are responsible for nurturing unity among the parishes and people of their dioceses and with the worldwide church. Bishops who commit themselves to supporting the ministry of lay parish leaders do so out of a conviction that such efforts will renew their dioceses "in the image of the church as a communion" and facilitate the genuine participation of all the baptized in the one ministry of Jesus Christ.

Institutional Support?

Ten years ago the Institute for Pastoral Life recommended that: "Dioceses should institutionalize adequate policies with respect to PLCs [parish life coordinators]. In particular . . . internships, coordination of diocesan and parish plans concerning PLCs, the role of the PLC in the context of all diocesan and parish ministries, and the place of the PLC in diocesan accountability" (Burkart, 1992: 129–130).

Yet the lay leaders and diocesan coordinators interviewed witness that such policies are still not the norm. Some dioceses welcomed the presence of lay leaders as a gift of the Spirit and now have sophisticated, respectful systems in place for including them in the pastoral care of the whole diocesan church. Others still treat lay parish leaders as a problem that, if ignored long enough, might just go away. Much of the evidence has already been cited from the point of view of the lay leaders. Now we will examine diocesan support from the perspective of the diocesan coordinators who were interviewed. Like Sister Charlotte, they seek to facilitate the ministry of lay leaders, but their efforts are sometimes thwarted by lack of time or imagination, unsupportive leaders, or entrenched organizational systems.

Appointment decision. How do dioceses decide where to assign lay leaders? One diocesan coordinator said that their determination is based on serving the greatest possible number of people with priest-pastors; thus, size of the parish is the prime factor. Another pointed to parish viability as the key factor. However, the range of parishes represented in this study indicates that it is no longer just the smallest and poorest parishes that receive lay leaders. There are good reasons for this.

Problems have become discernible in the practice of wedding the appointment of lay leaders to the size or financial viability of parishes. First, it displays a blatant preferential option for the richest and strongest parishes, who *always* receive priest-pastors. Second, it favors the clergy, allowing the ordained to receive the most delectable appointments before distributing the leftover scraps to lay leaders. Third, it can create a second class of "oppressed" parishes whose rights are chronically ignored and whose existence becomes invisible without priest-pastors to represent them in diocesan governance. Fourth, it can perpetuate the unhealthy tendency to write off parishes that have lay leaders because they are, after all, as good as gone. Fifth, it can marginalize lay parish leaders from the mainstream of diocesan life. Thinking of Marie Antoinette's famously insular reply, "Let them eat cake!" when told the people did not have any bread to eat, one can easily imagine Catholics in affluent parishes asking, "Priest shortage? What priest shortage?"

Several of the dioceses represented here are seeking to counteract some of these inequities. One coordinator said that their appointment decisions rest more on community needs and readiness than on numbers or finances. They consult with parishes to match the real needs of communities, regardless of size, with the gifts of those available, both lay and ordained. Another diocese rotates lay leaders through all the parishes in the diocese. In at least one diocese, parishes themselves have requested and received lay leaders. Sometimes a layperson is appointed to the parish with the most healthy and vital community life, one that can continue to flourish without an ordained pastor. While, in general, a bishop's decision to appoint laypeople to lead parishes in the diocese springs from a shortage of available priests, the reason for any particular appointment is always unique.

Appointment and transition process. It has already been noted that parish participation in the appointment and transition process facilitates the ministry of lay leaders. The Institute for Pastoral Life study found that: "Acceptance of PLCs is related to the manner in which the diocese manages PLC assignments in parishes, such as making PLC plans known to parishioners, selecting parishes according to this plan and giving parishes adequate time to prepare for their PLCs" (Burkart, 1992: 103). One coordinator interviewed said their diocese still has no such plan, whereas others indicated that there is at least some process in place. A well-developed process for parish involvement has already been described. As Sister Charlotte suggested, dioceses would be wise to also follow up with parishes that have lay leaders and seek their evaluative input. It would bring the transition process full circle, allowing the diocese to integrate the experience of each new parish involved.

Public recognition. Commissioning rituals have been seen to communicate authorization, respect, and gratitude for the ministry of lay leaders. Yet this is not the only way to recognize the contribution that lay leaders are making to the life of their dioceses. Some dioceses represented here do more. Visible participation in diocesan liturgies, such as ordinations, the Chrism Mass, and the Rite of Election, is a clear symbol of their dignity and their value to the diocese.

Visibility is also at issue in efforts to update diocesan language and communication, offices, and events to account for the presence of lay leaders. Publicity that shares the "good news" about the work they are doing allows the whole diocese to celebrate the vocation, dedication, and fruitfulness of the ministry of lay leaders. When bishops and diocesan officials speak to and about lay leaders publicly, rather than shrouding their ministry in silence, both lay leaders and their parishes regain their rightful sense of self-worth while the diocesan church awakens to the collaborative nature of the church's work.

Support for lay leaders. We have seen that dioceses can support lay leaders in a variety of ways. These include peer support groups, ongoing formation, supervisory relationships, legal and financial guidelines, and personnel policies that clearly delineate roles for lay parish leaders, sacramental ministers, and canonical moderators. Such support systems are so crucial that they merit constant collaborative evaluation and updating.

Dioceses cannot relinquish their responsibility for the financial support of lay leaders. Here the church's commitment to social justice is tested. Diocesan offices and sociologists who track changes in church practices insist that remuneration for lay leaders has improved dramatically in the last twenty years, yet most of those interviewed say they are struggling. Dioceses commonly set standards whereby lay leaders' packages are to match those of priest-pastors, while individual parishes are usually responsible for negotiating with and paying the lay leaders. In practice, this means that some parishes are too poor to hire a lay leader at all and some lay leaders, after financing their own graduate education, work for less than they deserve. To exacerbate the situation, their jobs are insecure, subject to changes in diocesan leadership and personnel policies in which they have no voice.

Canon 231.2 declares the right of lay workers in the church to receive appropriate remuneration and benefits. In *Called and Gifted for the Third Millennium*, the United States bishops also recognize the need to provide a living wage to lay ministers (*CGFTM*, 17). Both justice and charity demand that dioceses find ways to assist impoverished parishes in paying just salaries to lay parish leaders.

Support for priests. In the document *Lay Ecclesial Ministry*, the United States bishops ask, "What kinds of formation and continuing education opportunities promote better relationships between lay and ordained ministers?" (*LEM*, 65). Perhaps the best way for a diocese to assist in massaging these sometimes strained relationships is to provide priests with the pastoral care and formation that they deserve. In the previous chapter we noted that ongoing priestly formation should foster a spirituality of communion for mission, openness to conversion, and hope for the future of the church, as well as the skills necessary for collaboration.

One coordinator also remarked that sheer exposure to one another is a significant means of breaking down barriers between lay and ordained parish leaders. Another said that, in spite of resistance from the presbyterate, their diocese now includes lay leaders at all the diocesan gatherings of "pastoral leaders." Lay leaders themselves believe that, while such participation isn't always comfortable, their presence at regional and other priests' meetings is helping build trust between priests and lay leaders.

Diocesan officials do well to encourage the presbyterate to take full advantage of gatherings of lay and ordained parish leaders as opportunities to eradicate attitudes that inhibit—and foster attitudes that support—collaboration. Ruth Wallace gives an example of a lay parish leader who "had been invited to make a presentation to the priests of the diocese [on how] to develop lay leadership in their parishes" (Wallace, 1992: 103). Every time lay and ordained leaders gather to play, pray, reflect on their faith, share experiences in ministry, and learn from one another, they build bridges on which they can stand together and join hands in genuine collaborative ministry.

"Consultative structures." Many of the lay leaders interviewed feel significant frustration with what they perceive to be "clericalism" in the institutional system. Before continuing it may be useful to clarify what precisely is meant by the expression "clericalism." Clericalism is not to be equated with the clergy. It is a preferential attitude toward those in the clerical state, a tendency toward which both lay and ordained Catholics can fall prey. Over the centuries it has contributed to the accretion of excessive status, privileges, power, and responsibilities to the clergy at the expense of the laity. Distinguishing between an appropriate and inappropriate balance of power between laity and clergy is an ongoing struggle for the church.

In the case of lay parish leaders, they often find themselves excluded from diocesan communication and decision-making networks. Since they find it difficult to stay connected with the presbyterate, they tend to focus their energies on the internal workings of their parish congregations. Granted, some diocesan priests also find themselves in this position, but the ordained have more choice in the matter. One diocesan coordinator described the danger of excluding lay leaders: "It pushes them into a congregational model of church," which is neither consistent with the tradition nor healthy for a Catholic parish.

Pope John Paul II has encouraged greater participation of the lay faithful in diocesan councils to "broaden resources in consultation and the principle of collaboration—and in certain instances also in decision making—if applied in a broad and determined manner." Referring to diocesan synods, councils, and episcopal conferences, he says, "These structures could contribute to Church communion and to the mission of the particular church"(*CL*, #25, 62–63). In *Lay Ecclesial Ministry*, the bishops also recommend "the appropriate incorporation of lay ecclesial ministers within the consultative structures of the diocese, particularly those lay ministers who are also parish life coordinators (appointed according to canon 517.2)" (*LEM*, 1999: 43). While approximately half of the lay leaders said they feel completely excluded from diocesan consultation, the others noted that consultative structures now include them, at least in part. How is this being done?

Because presbyteral councils are legally governing bodies in the church, lay people cannot sit on them. However, in one diocese the diocesan pastoral council now consults on all decisions having to do with parishes. In that diocese only questions having to do with priestly life are reserved exclusively to the presbyteral council. Another diocese has expanded its time frame and procedures for consultation to be certain that lay leaders are heard and integrated. In these dioceses lay leaders are able to offer the presbyterate a different perspective on the problems and needs facing the church and act as credible advocates for constituencies that might otherwise go unnoticed. Although they have no decision-making authority, and clerical circles retain governing power, the voices of lay leaders are influencing diocesan policy and reforming the system from within.

Communication networks. Presbyteral networks of communication present a separate problem. As with any fraternity, the brotherhood of priests is committed to nurturing a sense of shared identity with and providing mutual support to one another. The priestly fraternity makes a valuable contribution by building community among the priests of the diocese. However, fraternal networks are known for excluding as well as they include. In this case it is the lay parish leaders who are excluded from the information that is shared and coalitions that are formed in this informal priestly network of communication. Diocesan leaders, and bishops in particular, can play a role here by developing personal relationships with lay parish leaders and challenging the clergy to include lay leaders in their relational networks. It requires strong leadership and a deliberate choice to broaden informal "consultative structures" until they no longer perpetuate "clerical privileges."

The creation of additional diocesan structures and policies is limited only by the courage, determination, and imagination of the people who are included in the process. Sofield and Juliano, for example, have suggested developing programs to sensitize and train ministers for collaboration, giving financial priority to collaborative initiatives and departments in the diocese, including collaboration as part of all diocesan formation programs, and strengthening methods of accountability for all parish leaders. Across the country there are diocesan leaders, like Sister Charlotte and her bishop, who are courageously collaborating to reform institutional systems so that they can better facilitate the work of lay parish leaders, foster collaboration between the laity and the presbyterate, and include all pastoral leaders in diocesan structures of communication and consultation.

Building Communion

Clearly, there is no uniform practice for implementing the ministry of lay parish leadership or fostering collaboration between lay and ordained pastoral leaders. Each diocese gradually develops structures and policies as the needs of lay leaders and the opportunities they offer the diocesan church crystallize. However, there are discernible principles guiding their efforts "to teach, to model, to challenge, and to establish the structures for facilitating collaborative ministry at every level of the church" (Sofield, 178). These principles find a spokesperson in Pope John Paul II.

Spirituality of communion. In his apostolic letter to close the Jubilee of the Year 2000, the Holy Father asks the church "to promote a spirituality of communion." "Communion, or koinonia, embodies and reveals the very essence of the mystery of the church." The pope challenges his readers "to make the church the home and the school of communion" (*NMI*, #42, 43). This provides a blueprint on which diocesan efforts to support collaboration can be based. The vision of the church as a communion of creative love can give bishops and diocesan officials the courage and determination to persist against strong resistance in the ardent task of institutional reform.

Mutual respect. Pope John Paul goes on to describe the spirituality of communion that emerges from contemplation of the mystery of the Trinity. "A spirituality of communion means an ability to think of our brothers and sisters . . . as 'those who are a part of me' [and] to see what is positive in others, to welcome it and prize it as a gift from God" (*NMI*, #43). Diocesan leaders who seek to build collaboration between lay and ordained leaders can begin by pouring the foundation of mutual respect for the equal dignity and value of all leaders, whether lay or ordained, and all parishes, rich and poor. They do this by molding policies, processes, and structures that effect what they signify— mutual respect for each person as a valued sister or brother in Christ.

Conversion. "A spirituality of communion means to know how to 'make room' for our brothers and sisters . . . and resisting the selfish temptations which constantly beset us and provoke competition, careerism, distrust, and jealousy." A spirit that welcomes the insights of others and the growth that their presence can bring to one's life is the skeleton on which true collaboration can be built. Without these girders and columns, the least quake might bring the building tumbling to the ground. Perhaps the most difficult task of diocesan leaders is creating supportive networks and processes that "make room" for such conversion to take place; but without them, the Holy

Father says, the "external structures of communion will serve very little purpose" (*NMI*, #43).

Participation. The pope writes that "the new century will have to see us more than ever intent on valuing and developing the forums and structures which . . . serve to ensure and safeguard communion." He calls for better use of "structures of participation" and "fruitful dialogue between pastors and faithful" (*NMI*, #44, 45). Here are the nuts and bolts, the insulation and drywall, the plaster and paint of collaboration. "Communion," "sharing," and "participation" all are translations of the same word in the Greek Bible—*koinonia*. Structures and systems that enable sharing (or participation) by everyone in communication, consultation, ministry, evaluation, and reform are the stuff of which sharing (or communion) in the church's life and ministry is built. They are the outward manifestation of the inward sharing (or communion) of all the baptized in the life of the Trinity.

Hope. "Go forward in hope!" the Holy Father concludes his letter to the church. "We can count on the power of the same Spirit who was poured out at Pentecost and who impels us still today to start out anew, sustained by the hope 'which does not disappoint' (Romans 5:5)" (NMI, #58). Only those who labor in hope can labor together. Those who labor in fear either cannot entrust any work to others or quit when the work seems dangerous. In hope, diocesan leaders can complete the building of collaboration by putting on collaboration themselves. They can lead by courageously utilizing the principles of collaboration, fearlessly entrusting others (and the Holy Spirit) with decisions and work that they might be tempted to control themselves. Hope frees and hope sustains them as they labor together, modeling collaboration to those they lead.

Sign and Source of Communion

The "spirituality of communion" can also guide the work of bishops in renewing the diocesan church "in the image of the church herself as a communion." Bishops need not rush in as heroes and reform the church single-handedly. They do not need to take sole responsibility for diagnosing the church's ills and providing the cures. But neither should they relinquish all authority to those above or below them in the hierarchy of the church. Ronald Heifetz would say that what the church needs bishops to do is to lead. The fictitious bishop whose remarks open this chapter typifies many American bishops who are taking the lead in this process.

Role of the bishop. Bishops are responsible for promoting what they represent—unity among the many parishes and people of their dioceses and unity with the many dioceses in the worldwide church. This unity is indeed comm-unity, a gathering together in mutual love of different persons, parishes, and dioceses to serve the needs of God's world. It is "a communion of communions. The bishops . . . not only sacramentalize this unity in their person and relationships, but their first pastoral concern is to preserve and promote that unity both in their own particular church and within the communion of churches" (Wood, 2000: 79).

How do bishops "sacramentalize" this image of the church as a communion? They represent, model, "preserve, and promote" the communion of the church. Bishops who wish to foster true collaboration, or communion, among the pastoral leaders of their dioceses can embrace four tasks that flow from their role of representing, modeling, preserving, and promoting communion. The list draws on Ronald Heifetz's understanding of true leadership and from John Paul II's understanding of the spirituality of communion.

Tasks of bishops. First, bishops can lead by naming the *vision.* Particularly in their public statements they can provide direction to the church by constantly unfolding the meaning of communion. They can challenge lay and ordained ministers to allow themselves to be converted into the image of communion by genuine collaboration in ministry.

Second, bishops can lead by *example.* All their words and deeds should model their commitment to participation, their profound respect for all ministers in the church as equals, their trust in the Holy Spirit, and their openness to conversion.

Third, bishops can lead by offering *encouragement*. They can offer people the security and protection that comes from knowing that collaboration is squarely within the tradition of the church and that the Holy Spirit is their guide and companion on the journey.

Fourth, bishops can lead by *reforming* structures, systems, and processes in their dioceses. They can provide order to the process of involving the people of their dioceses in participating in, critiquing, and rebuilding the diocesan church "in the image of the church as a communion." By promoting structures and habits of communion, their legacy will outlast the short time that they have to serve as bishops of their dioceses.

A model of episcopal ministry. This is precisely what Cardinal Mahoney, Archbishop of Los Angeles, is doing. It is noteworthy that the named author of his pastoral letter on ministry is "Cardinal Roger Mahoney and the Priests of the Los Angeles Archdiocese." He did not simply write, or commission someone to write, the letter. He led by gathering the priests of the diocese to discern together what should be said and done to foster collaborative ministry. In the letter he "pledges his support to the priests, religious and laity as we move forward together to meet the needs of our local church, working together to reshape ministerial structures so that they allow for a more collaborative and inclusive exercise of ministry" (*Origins*, May 4, 2000: 752). To that end he gives the readers concrete exercises and questions to help everyone participate in evaluating current practice in the light of the firmly grounded teaching in his letter. Finally, the cardinal is "convoking an archdiocesan synod, which will include members of the whole people of God" on the topic of collaboration in ministry (Mahoney, 753).

Leaders like Cardinal Mahoney show the way and provide real hope that collaborative ministry based on the image of the church as a communion has the power to reform the church from within.

The Communion of All the Baptized

All Catholics are called to deeper communion with one another within their parishes, in their dioceses and the universal church, and in the societies in which they "participate." The principles of collaboration between lay and ordained ministers can serve as a model of what is necessary for *all* the baptized to more fully reflect the image of the church as a communion. These principles take us back to the words of Pope John Paul II on the spirituality of communion. It is a spirituality of mutual respect, of welcome and conversion, of "participation" and inclusion. It is a spirituality of hope that propels the church forward until the whole world "participates" in God's creative love.

Such a spirituality invites *all* the baptized to participate. This means not being afraid to entrust decisions and work to others, or to take responsibility for one's share. It means celebrating often and well the beauty and achievements of others, and fully valuing oneself. It means welcoming new ideas, and offering critique in love and hope. It means seeking others' wisdom before making decisions, but making them nonetheless. It means fostering relationships built on understanding. It means seeking out those who may be forgotten. It means seeking support and seeking justice. It means making time to play and pray with others. It means never settling for the status quo just because change is threatening. It means coaxing others out of their individualistic habits and continually inviting oneself to enter more deeply into communion with humankind.

The pope begins and ends his words on communion with reference to chapter five of Paul's letter to the Romans. There Paul says, "We boast in our hope of sharing the glory of God . . . and hope does not disappoint us, because God's love has been poured into our hearts through the Holy Spirit that has been given to us" (vv. 2, 5). The church's sharing in God's love through the Holy Spirit leads the baptized to the confident hope of sharing *(koinonia)* at last in the fullness of God's glory. Thus, the love of God that lives and works through the communion *(koinonia)* of the baptized here and now will not fail to extend that sharing *(koinonia)* in God's love to the whole world.

These words can encourage *all* the baptized to imitate Sister Charlotte and her bishop by following the blueprint of communion in their homes, at work, in parish committees, classes and choirs, in diocesan structures, and in every cluster of human society in which they "participate." Such construction will be cemented in mutual respect for every beloved sister and brother, girded by openness and conversion, and built with the nuts and bolts of inclusion and participation. Whether ordained or not, every one of the baptized who chooses to work in communion rather than work alone or give up in despair leads others to participate more deeply in the profoundly creative love of God.

Questions to Consider

- If your parish were to receive a lay parish leader, how would you want to be involved in the process?
- How can dioceses increase lay leaders' sense of "job security?"
- What might your diocese do to foster collaboration between lay and ordained parish leaders?
- What are the consultative structures in your diocese? How are laypeople included?
- What aspects of a "spirituality of communion" do you find most challenging? What aspects do you find most attractive? Explain.
- How have you experienced your bishop as a leader? What would you like him to do?
- What discourages you about the church? What gives you hope and courage?

✺ CHAPTER 8 ✺

What's Next?
Trusting the Spirit

When Denise joined the group for coffee and donuts, I couldn't believe how energetic and beautiful she looked. I never looked that good after a long Sunday morning at church! I watched her move around the room touching everyone she talked to, laughing often and heartily.

"Good morning, Denise. I'm Virginia Stillwell."

"Yes. Welcome. I had a hard time finding you amongst the regulars. You fit right in here."

"That's because everybody made me feel at home."

"Did you enjoy the liturgy?"

"Very much. Thoroughly traditional, yet filled with the spirit of this community."

"Just what I like to hear. Let's go for a walk. I need to wind down a bit."

"Sounds wonderful. I appreciate your letting me interview you. I only have a few questions, actually. I already have lots of information. It shouldn't even take half an hour."

"Shoot."

"You're in your third year here, aren't you? How has it been for you, Denise?"

"This is the toughest ministry I've ever done. You have to be pretty centered and know who you are and stand your ground. You have to have a lot of faith and love the church. But the rewards are great. The growth in the parishioners' lives and their participation in the liturgy give me life and joy. Spiritually, people have touched my life in many ways. They're shaping me at the same time that I'm shaping them. I've been gifted by the people here."

"What do you find are the greatest challenges for you in this ministry?"

"Various things. The energy. Being on call 24/7. Balancing private renewal time with work is my biggest struggle. It's also hard to keep the broad vision I need in order to do the job. I can't possibly know all the answers, but I should know the resources. There's church politics, nasty, uncooperative people, but there's a lot of good that happens in the church and, well, the Gospel is worth it."

"Do you have any concerns about laypeople leading Catholic parishes?"

"I am concerned that the sacraments may not mean as much as they could if the one presiding was the pastor of the parish. There was a woman who became Catholic, and I did all the preparation with her. She said that I was the one who represented the community, not the priest. That was difficult.

"I'm concerned that the men and women who lead parishes are made to feel we are 'better than nothing.' I'd like the church to get to the point of saying, 'These people are blessed with these gifts and we are so happy.' I'm concerned that the church still doesn't financially support the education of lay ministers and we work for less than we deserve. My deepest concern is whether this ministry enables the male celibate clergy and an unhealthy system to continue—the unhealthiness being the sexism and the clericalism within our church. It gets down to the discussion of whether the clerical system is so broken that it can't be fixed and should be allowed to fall apart."

"Some people see the appointment of lay parish leaders as a regrettable necessity; others see it as a providential opening. What are your thoughts on this?"

"Some of my sisters in Christ see this as filling in slots, working against the ordination of women. They say the church should be deprived until Rome acts. I don't agree. In the meantime it's the people who would be deprived. I minister to people's needs. It's unbelievable how many people have come back to the church through my ministry. I feel if I wasn't here this wouldn't have happened. It would be a sin to deny the faith and the needs of these people. Many more people are being served than if we weren't here. So I don't think it's regrettable.

"One of the providential things about lay parish leaders is that communities experience women and married men in leadership. In many other denominations women can't do anything. It has made me realize how much Catholic women can do. And it's opening the door slowly. When people see us as capable they start asking why we can't be ordained. I feel I'm called to prepare the people of God to imagine others in leadership so that, if they are ordained, the church will be ready; and we will have, not a backlash, but a welcome party."

"Do you encourage other people to enter this ministry?"

"Definitely. We are on the leading edge; we are the future of the church. But only if someone has a vocation and the maturity for parish leadership. I know the hardships involved. Also, in some dioceses there's not much future for lay parish leaders. I do encourage people to go into lay ministry, to take their leadership of the church seriously. I talk to folks about using their gifts as a layperson. I become upset when vocations are discussed and lay ministries are never mentioned. How can we call forth from everyone the best that their gifts can offer, without focusing entirely on ordination?"

"What other insights would you like to share?"

"I believe so much that people need pastoral leadership, that it doesn't matter what the leader's status is—the people need leadership. Their needs and rights are more important than one person's status. I've experienced my ordination among the people I serve. They don't feel I'm 'better than nothing.' They're proud of who their leader is. We've created something that helps the church realize that we are one, with one mission. Our status shouldn't come first. Baptism is our call to ministry.

"This ministry is a logical progression of Vatican II and we sure need it at this time in our history. It has educated both the laity and the clergy. It has broadened people's vision of the church and ministry and the role of women in the church. But we don't have a plan all worked out. It's a sacred plan that's unfolding and we're trying to steward it. We don't know what will come of all of this. I pray that we can continue to be faithful to the Holy Spirit as the process unfolds."

"Thank you for your time and honesty, Denise. And thanks for your love of the church and openness to the Spirit."

"*Deo gratias.*"

ɔ̃

*T*hroughout this book the characters of Denise and Stephen have "spoken for" the lay leaders who were interviewed. The lay leaders' words that are quoted in this last conversation convey their heavy yet hopeful sense of the impact their ministry is having on the life of the church. Their concerns for the future focus on the place of the sacraments in Catholic life, the question of ordination, and continued "clericalism." Their vision for the future pictures ministry that flows from needs rather than status in a church where all the baptized recognize their vocation and take responsibility together for the priestly, prophetic, and pastoral ministry of Christ. *All* the baptized—both ordained and ordinary—can learn from the witness and vision of lay parish leaders. It is a vision propelled by confident hope that the Holy Spirit's power and guidance are efficaciously present in our day in the communion of God's holy people.

The Attitude of Lay Parish Leaders

Specific experiences of lay parish leaders have provided the basis for every chapter in this book. It only remains for us to identify the overall attitude these leaders have toward their experiences in ministry. As was already mentioned, most of those interviewed feel the same internal challenges that priests and others in full-time ministry feel. They struggle to find time, money, and energy, to keep balance in their lives, to find volunteers, to protect boundaries and set limits. They sometimes feel isolated by their work. All these challenges are amplified for those who sense that both the hierarchy and the parishioners see them as "temps"—just filling in until Father gets back.

Yet the lay leaders interviewed also reap bountiful spiritual rewards from their ministry. They say that they receive personal satisfaction and support from their parishioners. It is both gratifying and energizing for them to witness the empowerment of the people in their parishes and the changes they see in the diocesan church. Their overall attitude is one of hopeful realism that recognizes the weight and the worth of their contribution to the life of the church.

Unresolved Concerns

The pastoral experience of these lay leaders raises significant concerns about the future of the church's sacramental practice. However, an unscientific, experiential study such as this cannot provide definitive answers to theological questions or solutions to sacramental dilemmas. Complementary studies of members of priest-less parishes and of priests who serve as sacramental ministers would help put into perspective the comments of the lay leaders, priests, and coordinators whom I interviewed here. Ongoing assessments of and reflection on the church's pastoral experience of this ministry will be needed. Still, the experience of those interviewed demands that we name and explore the unresolved issues presented by their ministry.

Sacraments. Many fear that the anomaly of laypeople leading parishes will diminish the centrality and power of the sacraments in the life of the church. The concern is that when Catholics have only limited access to the sacraments, they will learn to do without the Eucharist and other sacraments. While this seems reasonable, there is little evidence to support this theory from countries where congregations celebrate Mass infrequently. In fact, their hunger and devotion seems only to increase.

Perhaps the analogy of the body might offer a useful counter-point to this concern. As the human body works harder and gets more exercise, it needs more food and drink. So too with the Body of Christ. As the baptized exercise their gifts more fully for the sake of the world, they have more to celebrate and require more spiritual nourishment to stay healthy and united. Rather than threaten the place of the sacraments in the life of the church, perhaps lay leadership actually increases a parish community's need for the sacraments by "building up" the "muscles" of the Body of Christ.

Susan Wood reminds us of a second reason for concern about the role of the sacraments in priestless parishes. This is the profound connection between presiding at the Eucharist and presiding *over* the life of the community: "Presidency refers to the ecclesial life of the community before it refers to a liturgical function" (Wood, 2000: 134). This explains the dissonance that lay parish leaders and parishioners sense when the leader of the parish does not lead the community at prayer. So the participation of the community in the sacraments may be compromised not only by their limited access to the Eucharist and other sacraments, but also by their limited relationship with the priest who presides.

Two very different conclusions can be drawn from this variance between the practice and the ideal. One is that laypeople should not lead parishes. Some people believe this is the case. If there is no ordained leader for the parish, it should be closed, clustered, or remain leaderless until a priest can be found. The people should be deprived of both sacraments and leadership. In this model the life and ministry of the church is seen as hinging on the presence or absence of an ordained Catholic in the community.

The second conclusion is that "Ideally, pastoral administrators should be ordained" (Fox, 1997: 247). Some people agree with this conclusion. If there is no ordained leader, a leader should be lifted up from the community and authorized by the bishop to preside over both its life *and* its liturgies. The people should not be deprived of either sacraments or leadership. In this model the life and ministry of the church is seen as hinging on the faith of the gathered community, independent of whether there is an ordained Catholic in their midst. This perspective leads us to the second concern—the question of ordination.

Ordination. Before the Vatican prohibited such discussion, many voices were raised in questioning the church's criteria for ordination. Among them were the voices of bishops from around the world— Africa, Asia, Indonesia, Europe, and the United States (Michel, *Pro Mundi Vita*, 1989: 43). They focused their attention on the discipline of celibacy, asking whether the thousand-year-old connection between priesthood and celibacy must continue. In the intervening years many theologians have also questioned the reservation of ordination exclusively to males.

It is clear that the criteria for priestly ordination in the Catholic Church will not change anytime soon. It is also clear that most of the lay parish leaders who were interviewed here have no desire to be ordained. Yet through their ministry Catholics are experiencing the capable and spiritual leadership of women and married men. What the future of ordination may be only the Spirit knows. For the present, the ministry of lay parish leaders is helping to refocus the attention of ordained and ordinary Catholics on the power and dignity of baptism.

A Vision for Ministry

Some people believe that lay parish leaders are merely propping up the crumbling walls of clericalism that can exclude the laity and imprison the clergy. Others fear just the opposite, that lay parish leadership will chip away at all that separates lay and ordained Catholics until the walls come tumbling down. The reality seems to be much less dramatic than either of these scenarios.

It is helpful to remember that clericalism is an excessive tendency toward which both lay and ordained Catholics are susceptible. Clericalism is no one's friend. It can do as much to obscure the distinct priestly identity of the ordained as it has done to obscure the common priesthood of all the baptized, and it does nothing to further the ministry of Jesus Christ. Perhaps this is the reason that the *Instruction* on collaboration clearly stated that its goal was not to "defend clerical privileges" but to safeguard the "pastoral ministry of priests"—two quite separate issues (*Instruction*, Conclusion).

Lay parish leaders are refusing to focus on anyone's *status* as "clerical" or "nonclerical." They are focusing on the *needs* of the church and the world. And they are focusing on how the baptized— lay and ordained together—can best participate in the pastoral ministry of Jesus Christ to serve those needs. The rights, responsibilities, and needs of the People of God are uppermost in their minds. While they often feel the negative effects of clericalist attitudes from both laity and clergy and worry that their ministry may be offering indirect support to clericalism, this is not stopping them from ministering to people's needs and calling forth people's gifts. While they recognize the limits of their status as "merely baptized," this is also not keeping them from providing people with the pastoral care and leadership they deserve.

This vision of ministry sets very clear priorities. The highest priority is the participation of *all* the baptized in the priestly ministry of Jesus Christ. This means that *meeting the needs* of the church and the world takes precedence over operating within the limits of anyone's status as "laity." It means that *embodying the image of the church as communion* through genuine collaboration takes precedence over protecting anyone's status as "clergy."

For centuries clerical privileges have obscured the common identity of the baptized. In this vision of ministry based on needs, not on status, clericalist tendencies lose their force in the face of the church's responsibility to continue the ministry of Jesus Christ. This vision is, indeed, chipping away at the walls of "clerical privileges." And when these walls finally crumble, both clergy and laity will be free to collaborate effectively for the life of the world, manifesting clearly the image of communion that Christ indelibly impressed upon his church.

This is a healthy vision for the future of ministry in a church that seems sure to have fewer priests serving greater numbers of Catholics.

It is a vision in which lay and ordained ministers collaborate as equals to welcome and cultivate the baptismal gifts of all Catholics so that together the church will bear rich fruit for a hungry world.

A Vision for All the Baptized

If "we are one, with one mission," and "baptism is our call to ministry," then "how can we call forth from *everyone* the best that their gifts can offer?" We can look one last time toward the example of lay parish leaders. Pope John Paul II has been quoted as saying "that these ministries do not transform lay persons into clergy, but that those who receive them must be considered as *archetypes of the participation of all the faithful in the salvific mission of the Church*" (Fox, 1995: 201, italics added). How can these nonordained Catholics lead every member of the faithful—lay and ordained—to participate more fully in the ministry of Jesus Christ? What can each Catholic learn from the ministry of the baptized leading the baptized?

Bishops. Lay parish leaders are not afraid to lead. But neither are they a threat to the ordained. They empower all the baptized to take responsibility for the life and ministry of the church. They facilitate collaboration as equals in the parish and seek to collaborate with the clergy. They challenge dioceses to account more completely for the participation of the merely baptized in structures of consultation and decision making as well as in leading the ministry of the church.

Bishops needn't be afraid to appoint lay leaders. Those who wish to serve the communion that they signify in their diocesan church will courageously appoint and support the ministry of these lay Catholics. They will lead their churches by allowing the image of the church as communion to permeate all they do, proclaiming it as the working principle on which every process, decision, ministry and structure in their diocese will be modeled. They will lead by empowering all the baptized—lay and ordained—to participate together in the collaborative ministry of Jesus Christ.

Diocesan Leaders. Lay parish leaders sometimes feel it necessary to challenge those in authority. Whether it is the bishops at whose pleasure they serve, the priests with whom they work, or the parishioners they lead, they will not keep silent about the need for conversion and reform in the church that they love. Reform takes hope and courage. It also takes endurance and needs a supportive hand. Lay parish leaders commit themselves for the long haul, to change the institution from within rather than criticizing it from outside the walls.

Those in diocesan leadership cannot shirk their responsibility to keep the pilgrim People of God moving forward on their journey. They know from experience that change comes slowly and only with resistance. Yet they must not be afraid to prophesy to the "king" and facilitate processes whereby evaluation and growth can take place. Beginning with an openness to conversion in themselves, they must willingly listen to all voices and respond with imagination and courage to what they hear. They must find ways to support the spiritual growth and ministerial collaboration of all pastoral leaders in the diocesan church.

Priests. Lay parish leaders are appointed to "participate" in the pastoral care of their parishes. Thus, collaboration is in their job description. They seek to collaborate with the clergy in pastoral leadership, each fulfilling a distinct task. They identify as equals with the people they lead, an attitude that breaks old patterns of dominance and dependence. Because they know how easy it is to become isolated and discouraged in their work, they seek support and nourishment from their collaborators in Christ.

Priests who seek a distinct priestly identity in a rapidly changing church can find self-definition as collaborators in leadership of the ministry of Jesus Christ. They can recognize all pastoral ministry as collaborative ministry. They can embrace their Christian identity as one among equals and discover the roots of their priestly vocation in the priesthood they hold in common with all the baptized. They are invited to build relationships of respect, support, and learning with other pastoral leaders and reach out as pastors to their lay brothers and sisters in ministry. They are urged to welcome all that the Spirit is doing through the merely baptized, confident that Christ's church can never be led too far astray.

Deacons. Lay parish leaders focus squarely on enabling parishioners to exercise their gifts in order to respond to the needs of their world. Service and ministry are foremost in their leadership of the church. While all administer parish affairs, many preach, and some preside at marriages, baptisms, and funerals, lay leaders do not see any of this as central to the task of pastoral care. Instead, they emphasize serving people's real needs out of the many graces that are available in the church.

It is easy for permanent deacons to become distracted from their ministry of *diakonia*. They are called on to fill so many gaps in the institutional church. Modeling themselves after lay parish leaders will keep their focus where it belongs. Ministry to the world is the mission of the church. Facilitating this ministry should be the focus of permanent deacons. They can do so through administration, teaching, preaching, and sacraments, but empowering the People of God to exercise their gifts in service for the life of the world is at the root of diaconal identity and should characterize their ministry.

Lay Parish Leaders. Lay parish leaders can find themselves rather alone in the dioceses in which they serve. They can narrow their gaze to the life and work of their own congregations. They withdraw from clerical circles if wounded once too often. They close their mouths if they feel they are singing to deaf ears. They lose heart when treated as "better than nothing," and become discouraged, wondering if all their work is worthwhile.

By looking up and out at the work of other lay parish leaders, they can realize the many graces that are flowing from their ministry. They are part of a communion of lay leaders throughout the country. Together they are reshaping the church by empowering the baptized to claim their full dignity and challenging the clergy to reform their working relationship with the People of God. They can rejoice in all that God has done and hope for all that the Spirit has yet to do through them. Such joyful hope will give them the courage to keep fostering connections with the ordained and strengthen them to continue leading all the baptized.

Lay Ministers. Lay parish leaders see themselves as working alongside the ordained to lead the church in carrying out its ministry. They do not understand themselves to be working under or for Father. They believe their job is not to *do* the ministry of the church, but to *facilitate* the ministry of the church. As gatherers, delegators, and stewards, they devote the bulk of their time to calling forth, forming, and supporting the baptized in their shared ministry of service.

Lay ministers who try to take on the ministry of the church themselves do no one any favors. They rob the community of its right and responsibility to participate in Christ's saving ministry. They pile their desks so high with tasks that they must bolt their doors and hide away to defend against even more work. Lay ministers are invited to unbolt their doors, carry their stack of tasks out into the assembly, and drop the burden of the church's ministry in the laps of parishioners, where this responsibility belongs. This requires that they spend their time supporting the parish in its work. They are invited to take their rightful place next to their pastor, as collaborators in guiding the ministry of the whole People of God.

Parish Volunteer Leaders. Lay parish leaders model a style of leadership and decision making that begins at the bottom, not the top. They take the time to identify the shared needs of the church and the community. Next they identify the gifts required to meet the needs and the people who possess them. And finally, they call forth those members of the community and support them in carrying out their ministry. They do not start with directives from above, but instead use such directives to guide the ministry of the local community.

Parish councils, committees, and working groups can take their cue from this style of leadership. Their goal should not be to discover what Father wants them to do and find the easiest, most efficient way to do it. They should not become so tied to hierarchical statements, official texts, and standard programs that they forget to name and serve the real needs of real people. They can learn to take time together to discern goals, needs, and gifts, realizing that the quickest methods seldom foster true communion among the members of the Body of Christ.

"Ordinary" Catholics. In this study we have repeatedly spotlighted lay parish leaders as role models for ordinary lay Catholics. They show, rather than tell, the baptized how to fully exercise the priesthood that they hold in common. They utilize their gifts with courage and hope. They value each member of the baptized (including themselves) as uniquely gifted and called by God for service. They extend a spirit of hospitality and solidarity, taking time to share others' joys and sorrows. They participate fully, actively, and consciously in Sunday liturgy and in parish life. They seek to include everyone in parish information, decision making, formation, community life, and ministries. They miss people when they are not present.

As apprentices to these lay parish leaders, ordinary Catholics can learn that they are the church. Without everyone's full, active, conscious participation in parish life, the church is impoverished and the world deprived. Each person has a priestly contribution to make. They can learn to "put an end to childish ways" and relate to their priests as capable, responsible adults (1 Corinthians 13:11). They can learn to value the support and ideas of others, to build relationships and to welcome new people into the life of the community. They can learn that time spent playing, praying, and working with other members of the baptized is time well spent. When they claim the power and authority of the priesthood they share with *all* the baptized, they discover that what serves others also nourishes them—real participation in the Body of Christ.

Trust in the Spirit

For centuries the baptized have been leading the baptized in a long procession of faith and ministry. In all these members of the Body of Christ the Spirit has been efficaciously present, leading the church in hope. Today, lay parish leaders join the procession of the baptized leading the baptized. They may not know the places the church will pass on the journey, but they do not need to know. For the Spirit is in the lead as they empower the church to minister to the needs of God's world.

Saint Perpetua and Saint Felicity provide fitting models as we close this exploration of the ministry of lay parish leaders. We can claim them as patron saints of all the baptized who take seriously their collaboration in the communion of the church as priests, prophets, and pastors. These two "merely baptized" African women were thrown to the beasts on March 7, A.D. 203. Felicity had just labored to give birth and Perpetua was a nursing mother. The *Martyrdom of Perpetua* tells the story of their priestly, prophetic, and pastoral deeds.

A vision of heavenly communion filled them with the joy and hope they needed to endure in witnessing their faith even unto death. While they were in prison, Perpetua's *priestly* prayers relieved her brother from his suffering in purgatory. Her *pastoral* pleading and loving embrace reconciled "Optatus the bishop and Aspasius the priest," who had separated into competing camps. From the middle of the arena her *prophetic* preaching exhorted others: "Remain strong in your faith and love one another. Do not let suffering become a stumbling block for you." Through their holy witness even the prison warden became a believer. The women "share in the Lord's suffering" in their deaths as "spouse of Christ," although not celibate, and "darling of God," although not male.

In baptism these ordinary Christian mothers were called, empowered, and authorized to claim their priesthood and lead others in the church to full participation in the saving ministry of Jesus Christ. In the end, the author of the account prays that their witness be a "source of encouragement to the Christian community" so that "new examples of courage" might spring up among the baptized, "witnessing to the fact that even in our day the same Holy Spirit is still efficaciously present."

The Holy Spirit truly is "efficaciously present" in the courageous witness of the baptized leading the baptized. With the lay leaders of today's parishes, may Saint Perpetua and Saint Felicity lead *all* the baptized to claim the vocation, authority, responsibilities, equality, collaboration, and communion of the priesthood they hold in common. Saint Perpetua and Saint Felicity, pray for us!

Questions to Consider

- How do you feel lay parish leaders are having the greatest impact on the church?
- Would your parish have less interest in the sacraments if you had a lay leader? Explain.
- Have you experienced what we call clericalism? If so, how?
- Can you remember a situation when people's needs took precedence over standard rules or expected roles? What was positive or negative about that experience?
- What have you learned from the baptized leading the baptized?
- How will your knowledge of the ministry of lay parish leaders affect your faith life?
- How is the Holy Spirit "efficaciously present" in the church today?

❧ *B*IBLIOGRAPHY ❧

Beal, John P., James A. Coriden and Thomas J. Green, eds. *New Commentary on the Code of Canon Law: An Entirely New and Comprehensive Commentary by Canonists from North America and Europe, with a Revised English Translation of the Code.* Commissioned by The Canon Law Society of America. New York: Paulist Press, 2000. ISBN 0-8091-0502-0.

Burkart, Gary P., Ph.D. *The Parish Life Coordinator: An Institute for Pastoral Life Study.* Kansas City, MO: Sheed & Ward, 1992. ISBN 1-55612-569-0.

Cameli, Rev. Louis. "Vatican II and the Ongoing Formation of riests in a New Millennium." *Origins* 30.45 (April 26, 2001), pp. 722–726.

Catechism of the Catholic Church. Image Books. New York: Doubleday, 1995.

Coriden, James A. *The Parish in the Catholic Tradition: History, Theology and Canon Law.* New York: Paulist, 1997. ISBN 0-8091-3685-6.

Fox, Zeni. *New Ecclesial Ministry: Lay Professionals Serving the Church.* Kansas City, MO: Sheed and Ward, 1997. ISBN 1-55612-984-X.

Heifetz, Ronald A. *Leadership Without Easy Answers.* Cambridge, MA: Belknap Press of the Harvard University Press, 1994. ISBN 0-674-51858-6.

John Paul II. *"Novo millennio ineunte." Origins* 30.31 (January 18, 2001), pp. 489–508.

———. *Post-Synodal Exhortation of John Paul II: The Lay Members of Christ's Faithful People: "Christifideles Laici."* Boston, MA: Daughters of St. Paul, 1988.

Killen, Patricia O'Connell. "Rural Pastoral Leadership II: The Priestless Parish." *Ministry in the Small Church.* David Andrews, C.S.C., ed. Kansas City, MO: Sheed & Ward, 1988. ISBN 1-55612-106-7, pp. 101–120.

Libreria Editrice Vaticana. Annuarium Statisticum Ecclesiae 1999 [Statistical Yearbook of the Church]. Vatican City: *Libreria Editrice Vaticana*, 2001.

Mahoney, Cardinal Roger and the Priests of the Los Angeles Archdiocese. "Pastoral Letter on Ministry: As I have Done For You." *Origins* 29.46 (May 4, 2000), pp. 741–753.

Martyrdom of Perpetua, The. Patricia Wilson-Kastner, et al, trans. University Press of America, 1981.

Metzger, Bruce M. and Roland E. Murphy, eds. *The New Oxford Annotated Bible with the Apocryphal / Deuterocanonical Books, New Revised Standard Version.* New York: Oxford University Press, 1994.

Michel, Ernest. "Sunday celebrations in the absence of a priest in Europe." *Pro Mundi Vita Studies* 12: "Parishes without a resident priest" (November 1989), pp. 28–34.

———. "Questions and perspectives." *Pro Mundi Vita Studies* 12: "Parishes without a resident priest" (November 1989), pp. 42–45.

Myers, Bishop John. "Older Priests Invited to Consider 'Senior Pries' Retirement Alternative." *Origins* 31.9 (July 19, 2001), pp. 165–168.

National Conference of Catholic Bishops. *Called and Gifted for the Third Millenium.* Washington, D.C.: United States Catholic Conference, 1995.

National Conference of Catholic Bishops Committee on the Laity. *Lay Ecclesial Ministry: The State of the Questions (A Report of the Subcommittee on Lay Ministry).* Washington, DC: United States Catholic Conference, 1999.

Official Catholic Directory, The. New York: P. J. Kennedy, 2001.

Schoenherr, Richard A. and Lawrence A. Young, with the collaboration of Tsan-Yuang Cheng. *Full Pews and Empty Altars: Demographics of the Priest Shortage in United States Catholic Dioceses.* Social Demography. Madison, WI: University of Wisconsin Press, 1993. ISBN 0-299-13690-6.

Schuth, Sister Katarina. *Seminaries, Theologates, and the Future of Church Ministry: An Analysis of Trends and Transitions.* Collegeville, MN: Liturgical Press, 1999.

Second Vatican Council. "Decree on the Apostolate of the Laity" *(Apostolicam actuositatem). Vatican II: The Conciliar and Post Conciliar Documents.* Austin Flannery, ed. Collegeville, MN: Liturgical Press, 1980, pp. 766–798.

———. "The Dogmatic Constitution on the Church" *(Lumen Gentium)*. *Vatican II: The Conciliar and Post Conciliar Documents*. Austin Flannery, ed. Collegeville, MN: Liturgical Press, 1980. pp. 350–423.

———. "The Pastoral Constitution on the Church in the Modern World" *(Gaudium et spes)*. *Vatican II: The Conciliar and Post Conciliar Documents*. Austin Flannery, ed. Collegeville, MN: Liturgical Press, 1980, pp. 903–1001.

Sofield, Loughlan, S.T. and Carroll Juliano, S.H.C.J. *Collaboration: Uniting Our Gifts in Ministry*. Notre Dame, IN: Ave Maria Press, 2000.

Vatican Congregation for the Clergy, et al. "Instruction On Certain Questions Regarding the Collaboration of the Non-Ordained Faithful in the Sacred Ministry of Priests." *L'Observatore Romano* (15 August 1997) Insert.

Vatican Congregation on the Evangelization of Peoples. "Instruction on Sending Abroad and Sojourn of Diocesan Priests from Mission Territories." *Origins* 31.9 (July 19, 2001), pp. 170–172.

Wallace, Ruth A. *They Call Her Pastor: A New Role for Catholic Women*. Albany, NY: State University of New York Press, 1992.

Wood, Susan K., S.C.L. "Prebyterial [*sic*] Identity within Parish Identity." *Liturgical Ministry* 10 "Sacred Orders" (Summer 2001), pp. 146–152.

———. *Sacramental Orders*. Lex Orandi Series, John D. Laurance, ed. Collegeville, MN: Liturgical Press, 2000. ISBN 0-8146-2522-3.